TIME-STYLE

Style-based Tools for Managing Priorities, Projects and Deadlines

by

Paul A. Douglas Ph.D.

BELFAST BOOKS

© Copyright 2012, by Paul A. Douglas
All rights reserved.
Printed in the United States of America

This publication may not be reproduced, stored in a retrieval system, or transmitted in whole or in part, in any form or by any means, (electronic, mechanical, photocopying, recording, or otherwise) without the prior written permission from the publisher. Requests for permission should be addressed in writing to Belfast Publishing, 93 S. Jackson Street, Seattle, WA 98104.

Library of Congress Control Number: 2010906708

Douglas, Paul A.

   Time-Style / Paul A. Douglas
   p. cm.
   Includes index
   ISBN 978-0-919917-40-8
   1. Time-management   2. Management   3. Self-help

I. Douglas, Paul A.

II. Title
HM132

This publication is produced to provide current authoritative information on the subject matter covered. It is sold with the express understanding that the author and/or publisher is not engaging in rendering psychological, legal, or other professional services. If legal, psychological, or other expert assistance is required, a competent professional should be sought.

Printing number
10 9 8 7 6 5 4 3 2 1

To My Mother Mary Douglas

A truly remarkable Irish woman who had style in everything she did.

Preface

The greatest weakness found in most traditional time and project management programs is that they offer a, "one-size-fits-all" system or approach, to a multifaceted and complex subject ignoring the critical role personal and management style plays in organizational effectiveness. As a result, they fail to provide practical and realistic solutions that might reasonably be implemented by disparate personality styles.

In this book I have attempted to address these weaknesses by integrating the behavioral styles model and the latest work done in the area of social intelligence with the best practices for planning, personal organization and the management of time.

This volume represents a comprehensive new approach to the subject, by presenting insightful, style-specific tools and techniques for managing your time, your projects and your life. Most importantly, by providing techniques that align with your natural style, you will experience less stress while you accomplish more than you thought possible.

In the pages that follow I will provide you with a clear understanding of the behavioral styles model and the core principles and specific techniques of behavioral synchronization. This book is intended to not only provide a standalone guide for increasing self and social awareness but also, and perhaps more importantly, to demonstrate how an understanding of these tools can provide organizational techniques that will really work – for you!

The behavioral styles model provides an important framework for understanding and reconciling individual differences, providing a dynamic model for individual and organizational growth and advancement.

The primary self-assessment instrument is the Individual Multidimensional Inventory & Normative Diagnoses (iMind^2), a construct utilized by many organizations large and small. TIME-STYLE will show you how to utilize this important tool to identify your personal time-style, and subsequently help you develop new and effective, individually personalized solutions to your major organizational and time-management problems.

My goal is to help you develop the "do-it now" habit ensuring the accomplishment of your highest priorities.

You will develop style-based techniques for handling interruptions, overcoming procrastination, and developing team relationships that build productivity. You will also discover new ways to set priorities and stick to them in crisis. Most importantly, you'll learn how to improve your personal effectiveness and still maintain a calm, controlled, stress-free approach to your objectives; because the techniques you will learn will fit your personality and unique time-style.

Paul A. Douglas
May 17th, 2012

Contents

Chapter 1

Taking Back Control

In 1950 Twentieth Century Fox released a film starring Clifton Webb and Myrna Loy entitled *Cheaper by the Dozen*. This film chronicled the life of Frank Gilbreth, one of the first and most celebrated "efficiency experts" in the United States and his large family of twelve children. In the early decades of the twentieth century there were many of these so-called scientific engineers or time-and-motion study men that were embraced by American industry because they showed how by measuring and altering the physical movements of workers productivity could be increased.

While Gilbreth was one of the leaders in the scientific management or industrial engineering movement, there were many like him that would go into factories and measure the wattage in the light bulbs, or the muscle strength of the workers, or the speed at which materials would travel down assembly lines. They would make recommendations to management on how to become more efficient by increasing the wattage of the light bulbs, hiring people with greater muscle strength, or changing the angle of levers. And for a time, these efficiency experts were very popular because they showed American industry how to increase bottom-line profits. Based on a book by Gilbreth's son, the film portrayed how Gilbreth brought his obsession with efficiency to the running of his large household. For example, when he arose in the morning, he would sound a whistle that hung around his neck and then time how long it took each of the children to trundle down to breakfast. Gilbreth knew exactly what time to leave for work in the morning so he would hit all the green lights, and at one point in the film, he is shown in the principal's office at one of the children's schools, demonstrating to the principal and teachers how you can take a bath in the time it takes to play one phonograph record, (three or four minutes) by moving the soap in a particular pattern over your body.

Well, a lot of people think that cramming more in is what time management is all about, about learning to pack more and more into every minute, and that success can only be achieved through greater efficiency.

While efficiency certainly is important, the real measure of success is effectiveness. The former may be defined as doing the job right in the shortest possible time, whereas the latter is defined as doing the right job.

Billions of dollars are spent each year in this country trying to help people become more efficient. Smart phones and iPads® and organizers and a myriad of software programs are heralding the benefits of greater efficiency while barely giving a nod to increased effectiveness.

Many of us spend a great deal of our time taking care of urgent trivialities, doing them efficiently, but too often neglecting the most important things in our lives, the things that really need to be done.

There are three types of activities that contribute to this misalignment of effort:

1. Unimportant Tasks
2. Unanticipated Tasks
3. Tasks Based on Other People's Priorities

Have you ever had a day filled with such tasks?

You come into your office an hour early because you have been chosen to give the welcoming address at your company's annual convention. Your speech is not for another month, but because of the visibility it will afford you and the possible benefits to your career, you have been coming in early as often as you can to be able to work on the speech without distraction and get a bit of a leg up.

When you arrive at your desk, however, you find a sticky note from your boss on your computer screen, which reads, "Call me as soon as you get in; I am in shipping." You pick up the phone and call your boss in shipping, and he informs you that a few railcars of your product, headed across country to your most important customer, have simply disappeared. You can hear the panic in his voice as he says, "The client has been on the phone to me already this morning and says that if his order is not received within 48 hours, they are going to have to cease production in their factory and there is going to be hell to pay." He continues, "If we lose our most important customer, head office will not be pleased. FIND THOSE RAILCARS!"

You say, "I'm on it," hanging up the receiver and then dialing your shipping agent. Three hours later, you have located the lost railcars. They are sitting on a sidetrack in Great Falls, Montana. Because of snow conditions, they had to uncouple a few cars and somehow had forgotten to send another engine to collect them. It takes you another ninety minutes to arrange to have a trucking company load the shipment and get it on the interstate so the product can be delivered to your client's docks directly before the close of business tomorrow.

It is 11:45 a.m. and you have forgotten about doing any preparatory work on your talk. You pick up your "to do" list, the one you had created before you went home the night before, but before you can even think about the first item, Sally from personnel pokes her head in and says, "Hi, I just wanted to pick up the envelopes."

"Damn," you think. You had forgotten you had promised you would collect your department's United Way contribution envelopes this year. You ask Sally, "When is the very latest I can get them to you?"

"Before I go home at 4:30 p.m., today," she responds.

The remainder of your morning and most of your afternoon is spent pinning down your co-workers and getting their contributions. When you approach your boss, he says, "Thank goodness you solved that hassle with the lost shipment. I can't tell you what head office would have said to me if I lost that account. I don't know what I would do without you? I can always count on you." He adds, "By the way, I have another small favor to ask you, no biggie, but I was supposed to speak to the Rotary Club on Saturday on the environmental impact of our new smelting process. You did most of the work on it and know at least as much about it as I do. Would you mind covering for me? My wife is on my case to do a family thing."

"How long would I need to speak?" you ask.

"Not very long, ten or fifteen minutes – forty at the most."

As you walk back to your office, after having agreed to your boss' request, you have a sinking feeling in the pit of your stomach. "What have I got myself into," you think.

At any rate you do accomplish a few items on your "to do" list, even though you are interrupted five times by the telephone and three times by drop–in visitors before you go home.

Have you ever had a day like that? Does every day seem like this one?

Can you see that there were three major occurrences in the scenario that reduced your effectiveness?

The first was the unanticipated event, the lost shipment. Now, it may have been unanticipated, but it very important and had to be responded to.

The second was the unimportant task. This was the collection of the United Fund contributions. I am not saying the United Fund is unimportant, but you likely got roped into collecting for the organization through your own inability to say no. Also, three months ago when you were asked to help, it was so easy to be magnanimous and volunteer. You may have thought to yourself back then, "I am swamped now, but in a month or two, I'll have the slate clean and have lots of time to fit this in." But nothing changes; you are just as busy today, and the promises you make come home to roost.

The third problem was your commitment to speaking in your boss's stead at the Rotary Club. That was not your priority; it was your boss's priority, but you made it your own.

These three events and your inability to anticipate them and deal effectively with them resulted in your time-management problems for the day. Similar events and responses are the reason for the majority of most people's time-management problems. That is why learning how to deal with unanticipated tasks, unimportant tasks, and tasks based on other people's priorities is so important.

What is Time?

What is time? When I ask this question at my public seminars, I usually get the response that it's hours or minutes or days or years. These are, however, only man-made measurements of time. Time is what the hours and minutes and days and years are measuring. But what is time really? Many great thinkers have grappled with a definition of time and not been altogether satisfied with the result. Isaac Newton said time was absolute, that time existed independent of and outside of all other dimensions. Albert Einstein said that no, you couldn't separate time from events, that events in fact make up the substance of time.

I believe the following definition is as good a definition for time as you will ever get:

> **"Time is the occurrence of events in sequence or succession, one after another."**

According to this definition, everything becomes an event. Reading this book is an event. Brushing your teeth this morning was an event. Breathing in and out are events. Time is the occurrence of these and all other events in series one after the other.

What is Management?

Now this is a lot easier, we are all involved in managing something be it people or projects or budgets or our own behaviors. What do managers do? They plan, they organize, they delegate, they oversee, but all of these functions can be lumped together under one term – they seek to control. When you try to manage something you seek to bring it within your control be it resources or budgets or people - or time.

Simply stated then our working definition for management is just that:

"Management is the act of controlling."

What is Time Management?

Now, if we define *time* as the occurrence of events in sequence, one after another, and *management* as the act of controlling, by simply bringing those two sub-definitions together, we have a definition of time management.

"Time management is the act of controlling events."

Can we control everything in our lives? No. Can we control anything in our lives? Yes, of course we all believe that we can control a great many things in our lives, but we cannot control everything in our lives. But it is not that simple. Besides our belief structure, which indicates that we can control certain things and not others, there is an objective reality in the world in which we live, which says, at times, yes we can control certain things and, at times, that we cannot control certain other things.

Sometimes our belief structure is in concert with the real world; sometimes it is not. Consider the model below:

The Control Matrix

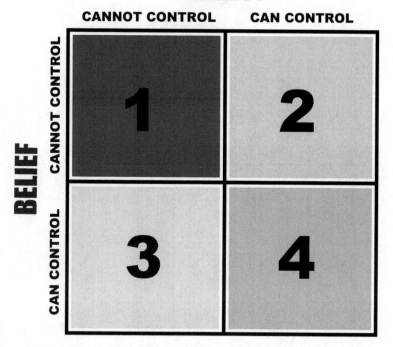

You'll note that on this matrix, there are four cells, a bipolar scale on which we measure reality on the X axis and belief on the Y.

Quadrant 1 is made up of those things that we believe that we cannot control and that we certainly cannot control. Can you think of something in your life that falls into that quadrant? The day you die? Would that fall into that quadrant? Not really. You have some control over the day you die by the way in which you live your life.

You don't have total control, of course, but you have some control. If you live a very prudent life, if you're careful about what you eat and drink, if you exercise, and if you don't enter into risky behaviors, you will likely survive longer than if you do the opposite—but there's no guarantee. You may get some terrible disease, or you might step off the curb and get hit by the bus. The weather would fall into this quadrant. Who your parents are, where and when you were born, the color of your skin; these things fall into the first quadrant.

What is the intelligent thing to do when we face events in Quadrant 1? Accept, adapt, roll with the punches, go with what you've got. As mortals, do we always do that? No. We fight, we kick, we fight against the slings and arrows of outrageous fortune, but it is all to no avail. These things are unchangeable. Life, it would seem, is not fair. In this book we're not going to spend a lot of time talking about Quadrant 1. You can't change who your parents were, your IQ, or most of your physical characteristics.

Look at Quadrant 2. This quadrant is more interesting to me. It contains those things in our lives that we feel we cannot control but we really can. Having taught seminars for nearly four decades now, and having taught at the university level before that, I have met and worked with thousands and thousands of people who have shared with me the ideas that they had for businesses they hoped to start, inventions they hoped to patent, careers they were going to change, relationships they were going to modify, and books they were going to write. But in the vast majority of cases, I have witnessed that those people have not gone on to do those things. Why? Because there is one thing that holds them back—the fear of failure. Many of us fail to do those things in our lives that we're perfectly capable of doing, sometimes eminently qualified to do, because we're afraid that we might fail. Yet anyone in this life who has ever accomplished anything significant has failed many more times than he or she has succeeded.

Thomas Edison, perhaps the most prolific inventor since the days of the great Leonardo, is a example. When Edison died, he had over 1,300 patents registered in the United States Patent Office. The vast majority of those patents went into material production, including inventions such as the tickertape machine, the phonograph, the first motion picture, and the incandescent light bulb under which you're probably sitting. Yet, it took Edison almost several years and more than 5,000 failed models before he got a light bulb to work. He was the laughingstock of his hometown during that time. A young reporter once caught up with him as he was coming off a train and said, "Tom, why don't you give up? If God wanted us to have light bulbs, he'd have hung them from trees." Edison's response was, "I haven't failed. I've found 5,000 ways how not to make a light bulb." He did hang in there and he did succeed. Let me read you the story of a political failure that you may recognize.

A Political Failure

1832 – Lost his job
1832 – Failed in business
1833 – Elected to legislature
1834 – Had a nervous breakdown
1835 – Sweetheart died
1836 – Defeated for the position of Speaker
1838 – Defeated for the nomination to Congress
1846 – Elected to Congress
1848 – Lost that nomination again
1849 – Rejected for a low-paying land officer job
1854 – Defeated for the Senate
1856 – Defeated for Vice-President
1858 – Again defeated for the Senate

But in 1860, Abraham Lincoln became the sixteenth President of the United States.

People who have ultimately succeeded haven't lived golden, charmed lives; rather, it's the tenacity that they've gained from getting up off the mat time and again that has resulted in the phenomenal successes at which we honor today.

I don't care who you are or what you are trying to do. I know that if you try to do something that takes you off the beaten path, there are going to be people lined up to tell you, first of all, why it can't be done and why, in particular, you can't do it.

I like to collect what I call timeless discouragements that demonstrate that, too often, well-meaning advice proffered by others is far off the mark.

"Forget it, Louis, no civil war picture will ever make a nickel."

That was Irving Thalberg talking to Louis B. Mayer when Mayer wanted to pick up the rights to Margaret Mitchell's *Gone With the Wind*, which I think you would agree went on to become a pretty successful flick.

Here's another one to do with the same film:

"*Gone with the Wind* is going to be one of the biggest flops in Hollywood history. I'm just glad it's going to be Clark Gable falling on his face and not Gary Cooper."

That was Gary Cooper in 1938. Cooper was first offered the role of Rhett Butler. I am sure he later regretted his decision.

"The Russians are finished. They have nothing left to throw against us."

That was Adolf Hitler talking to General Franz Halder in July of 1941, and if you know anything about the Second World War, it was the Russian campaign that turned the tide for the Nazis.

"I tell you, Wellington is a bad general, and the English are bad soldiers. We'll have this matter cleared up by lunchtime."

That was Napoleon Bonaparte talking to his generals before the decisive battle of Waterloo.

"You ain't going nowhere, son. You might as well go back to driving a truck."

That was Jim Denny, the manager of the Grand Ole Opry, when he fired Elvis Presley after his first and only performance there. September 25th, 1954. Did he go on to have a reasonable career?

"1930 will be a splendid employment year."

That was the US Department of Labor in 1929, the first year of the Depression.

"The world will little note nor long remember what we say here today."

That was, of course, Abe Lincoln dedicating the National Cemetery at Gettysburg in 1863.

"The army is the Indian's best friend."

That was General George Armstrong Custer in 1870.

"I would have made a good pope."

That was Richard Nixon in 1980.

Here's my own personal favorite:

"With fifty foreign cars already on sale here, the Japanese auto industry isn't likely to slice that much of a market in America."

That was *Business Week* magazine in 1958. Are there a few Japanese cars out there?

"I think there's only a world market for five computers."

That was Thomas Watson, the chairman of IBM in 1943.

Other people may think that they know better than we do about what we are capable of. But they don't.

Have you ever gone to a circus and noticed that as the animals come out into the ring, they're usually tied together in some way? They may be shackled or chained together, but they are usually simply roped together with a little white nylon rope. There's a manacle on the leg of one elephant, with this rope running to the manacle on the leg of the animal behind it.

Years ago, I took my young daughter, Elyse, to the Shrine Circus and as the elephants came out into the ring, she drew my attention to the fact that they were all tied together with what she called a "string." She said, "Daddy, why don't they break that string and run off and play?" I gave her question some thought, "Why don't they break that string and run off and play?" Here's a 10,000-pound elephant tied to the one behind it with a little white nylon rope.

I asked someone who knew about the training of animals, "Why don't they break it?" He said, "The reason they don't break it is they don't believe they can."

I said, "Well, of course they can break it." He said, "I believe they can and you believe they can, but the elephant doesn't believe it can. Why? Because when we train that young elephant, we put a steel manacle on its leg, and we weld a heavy gauge steel chain onto that manacle and we tie that chain to a brick wall." He continued, "For about three weeks on average, 21 days, that young elephant will tug and tear and pull and try to break free." Can it? No. But he explained that after about 21 days on average, it will stop trying. Why? Because at that point, the elephant's belief structure tells it that if there's something tied to its leg, it cannot break free of it, and, from that point on, for the rest of that animal's life, it won't try to break free. That's how powerful belief is.

I guess the question here is, is there some imaginary chain holding you down? Have you convinced yourself—or, worse yet, have you allowed others to convince you—that you're incapable of doing something that you're probably perfectly capable of doing and, in some cases, eminently qualified to do? I think you need to look at that again.

Some of us were told by a teacher back in Grade 3 that we were no good at math and we have repeated this mantra to ourselves all this time. "No, I don't like finance, I am not good at math." Maybe we need to revisit such beliefs.

Quadrant 3 on our control matrix is made up of those things that we believe we can control but, in reality, we cannot. There's one big group of things that fall into Quadrant 3—other people. You can't control other people. You can't control your kids, you can't control your spouse, you can't control your subordinates. Yes, you can influence their behaviors. Yes, you can modify their behaviors. Yes, you can encourage them, and you can certainly discourage them, but you cannot control them.

If you live your life trying to control other people, you're going to meet with failure. You're going to have very unsuccessful relationships.

Quadrant 4 is made up of those things that we believe we can control and that we can, in fact, control, but I have separated Quadrant 4 into two parts—4A and 4B. The 4As are those things that we believe we can control, that yes, in reality, we can control but we don't. Why not? Because, we don't know how! That's why people are interested in time management. There must be some way to better control, or at least shorten, my interruptions; there must be some way to say NO and make it stick without feeling guilty; there must be some way to overcome my tendency to procrastinate, deal with my failure to delegate, or control my perfectionism. Yes there is; in fact, this is what we focus on in the pages that follow.

Finally, there are the 4Bs. These are the things that we believe we can control, and that, in reality, we can and do control. What happens to your self-esteem when you experience the 4Bs? It soars. This is what we want more of.

So this provides for us a frame of reference for the work that we need to do.

Does the control matrix seem vaguely familiar?

If you are a friend of Bill W. or have ever been in recovery, you're familiar with the Serenity Prayer:

"God grant me the serenity to accept the things I cannot change, the courage to change the things I can; and the wisdom to know the difference."

God grant us the serenity to accept the things we cannot change (that's Quadrants 1 and 3), the courage to change the things we can (that's Quadrants 2 and 4), and the wisdom to know the difference.

Many of us lack that wisdom.

Chapter 2

Assessing Your Current Position

We have defined time management as the act of controlling events. Perhaps we might want to start our journey by examining how well you are presently controlling events.

In this chapter, you will be asked to complete the **Comprehensive Time Management Assessment (CTMA)**, which is designed to help you to identify those areas that you are managing well and those areas that need improvement.

For each of the 120 statements below, please circle a number between 5 and 1 according to the following criteria:

5 – I agree strongly with the statement
4 – I agree with the statement
3 – I am neutral with regard to this statement
2 – I disagree with this statement
1 – I disagree strongly with this statement

Please read each statement carefully and answer honestly in terms of how things are, not how they should be.

Comprehensive Time-Management Assessment

Instructions: For each of the statements that follow, please circle the number that best represents your behavior or belief, according to the scoring criteria below. If you feel that a statement does not apply to you, circle the number three (3) do not leave it blank. Please be completely honest, scoring yourself as you are, rather than how you would like to be, or what you might feel is right or correct.

SCORING CRITERIA:	1 - STRONGLY DISAGREE 2 - DISAGREE 3 - NEUTRAL 4 - AGREE 5 - STRONGLY AGREE				
1	I set aside a portion of each day to think, create and plan.	1	2	3	4	5
2	I use goal setting to decide which tasks and projects I should be working on.	1	2	3	4	5
3	I put my "to do" list on paper or enter into my electronic organizer each day.	1	2	3	4	5
4	I regularly confirm my priorities with my boss.	1	2	3	4	5
5	I choose to do my most important tasks when I am most alert.	1	2	3	4	5
6	I prioritize my "to do" list or action plan and note the time each task will require.	1	2	3	4	5
7	I have taken the time to establish and write down my life-time goals.	1	2	3	4	5
8	I tackle tasks in the order of their importance - not their urgency.	1	2	3	4	5
9	I know the hours of the day when I do my best work and schedule accordingly.	1	2	3	4	5
10	Given a new assignment, I determine it's importance and prioritize accordingly.	1	2	3	4	5
11	I have all of my contacts and phone numbers in one place.	1	2	3	4	5
12	My desk or other work surfaces are tidy; I can find what I need immediately.	1	2	3	4	5
13	Someone looking at my desk and it's drawers would say I am well organized.	1	2	3	4	5
14	My computer files and folders are well organized, and I have few unread emails.	1	2	3	4	5
15	When I need to locate paperwork from months before, I can find it very quickly.	1	2	3	4	5

Comprehensive Time-Management Assessment

SCORING CRITERIA:	1 - STRONGLY DISAGREE	2 - DISAGREE	3 - NEUTRAL	4 - AGREE	5 - STRONGLY AGREE
16	In my absence, someone could find a specific file within a minute or two.	1	2	3	4	5
17	I use a daily planner (book or electronic) to keep track of what I need to do.	1	2	3	4	5
18	I have a place for everything and everything is always in it's place.	1	2	3	4	5
19	I unsubscribe myself from anything that is no longer relevant to me.	1	2	3	4	5
20	I use my travel or waiting time well, I always have something to do with me.	1	2	3	4	5
21	I rarely find my time being wasted by drop-in visitors.	1	2	3	4	5
22	I am able to deal bluntly with people who want to waste my time.	1	2	3	4	5
23	Distractions and interruptions seldom keep me from working on critical tasks.	1	2	3	4	5
24	When someone pokes their head in my door with, got a minute?" I often say "No."	1	2	3	4	5
25	If my coworkers are noisy while I am trying to work, I will ask them to be quiet.	1	2	3	4	5
26	I let others know ahead of time I have a really busy day and can't be interrupted.	1	2	3	4	5
27	I limit the channels people use to distract me - turning off cell, work from home, etc.	1	2	3	4	5
28	When I have something very important to do, I will close my door.	1	2	3	4	5
29	Whenever I experience an interruption, I demonstrate a "get to the point" style.	1	2	3	4	5
30	When interrupted by something that needs my involvement, I try to postpone it.	1	2	3	4	5
31	I have my assistant screen my telephone calls (or I would if I had one).	1	2	3	4	5
32	I set blocks of time during the day when I will, and will not, answer the telephone.	1	2	3	4	5

Comprehensive Time-Management Assessment

SCORING CRITERIA: 1 - STRONGLY DISAGREE 2 - DISAGREE 3 - NEUTRAL 4 - AGREE 5 - STRONGLY AGREE					
33	If the phone rings while I am working intensely on a task, I let it go to voicemail.	1	2	3	4	5
34	I "batch" my outgoing telephone calls placing them in a single block of time.	1	2	3	4	5
35	If a telephone caller is long-winded I have no trouble assertively terminating the call.	1	2	3	4	5
36	I rarely feel the urge to socialize before or after the business part of a call.	1	2	3	4	5
37	I don't feel naked without my cell phone and often leave it behind on purpose.	1	2	3	4	5
38	I always prepare a brief rough outline before I place an important business call.	1	2	3	4	5
39	On the phone, I'm likely to ask, "What can I do for you?" rather than "How are you?"	1	2	3	4	5
40	It is rare for me to call someone back because I forgot something in my first call.	1	2	3	4	5
41	If I am working on something important I always ignore email alerts.	1	2	3	4	5
42	I have a strong spam filter and delete, unopened, emails from unknown senders.	1	2	3	4	5
43	I do not spend time on social networking sites - certainly never at work.	1	2	3	4	5
44	I resist placing personal emails or surfing the internet when I am at work.	1	2	3	4	5
45	I check my emails at certain times during the day rather than randomly or repeatedly.	1	2	3	4	5
46	It is rare that I go to news, sports or fashion internet sites while in the office.	1	2	3	4	5
47	When I open up my web browser, I do not first see: MySpace, YouTube or Facebook.	1	2	3	4	5
48	I only handle an e-mail once. - open it, reply to it or delete it.	1	2	3	4	5
49	I use a signature template and also have a 'proper use' warning on all my emails.	1	2	3	4	5

Comprehensive Time-Management Assessment

SCORING CRITERIA: 1 - STRONGLY DISAGREE 2 - DISAGREE 3 - NEUTRAL 4 - AGREE 5 - STRONGLY AGREE					
50	I try to put the purpose of my email in the subject line, "AP Meeting Tuesday 2 pm."	1	2	3	4	5
51	I rarely find myself completing tasks at the last minute, or asking for extensions.	1	2	3	4	5
52	I am not stressed about deadlines or the commitments I have made to others.	1	2	3	4	5
53	I seldom delay or put off hard decisions.	1	2	3	4	5
54	I am not afraid to ask people for more information.	1	2	3	4	5
55	I do not sidestep uncomfortable priorities.	1	2	3	4	5
56	I seldom start things that I don't finish.	1	2	3	4	5
57	I honestly do not have regrets over goals that I wished I had accomplished.	1	2	3	4	5
58	I do not back away from tasks because there's a good chance of failure.	1	2	3	4	5
59	I have not put off personal goals (e.g. writing a novel, starting a business, etc.)	1	2	3	4	5
60	I never put off tasks because they are daunting or uninteresting.	1	2	3	4	5
61	I pay as many of my utility bills, etc., as possible, by automatic on-line payment.	1	2	3	4	5
62	I recycle junk mail immediately and throw out magazines rather than hoard them.	1	2	3	4	5
63	I cancel my subscriptions to newsletters and magazines I no longer read.	1	2	3	4	5
64	I handle most incoming paper immediately, rather than put it in a pile.	1	2	3	4	5
65	I really do adhere to, and practice, the credo "If in doubt, throw it out."	1	2	3	4	5
66	At least yearly, I destroy files - paper and email that are no longer necessary to keep.	1	2	3	4	5

Comprehensive Time-Management Assessment

SCORING CRITERIA:	1 - STRONGLY DISAGREE 2 - DISAGREE 3 - NEUTRAL 4 - AGREE 5 - STRONGLY AGREE					
67	I scan and store correspondence and receipts electronically.	1	2	3	4	5
68	I have my mail sorted and pre-categorized by my administrative professional.	1	2	3	4	5
69	I request routine written staff reports less frequently, opting for verbal updates.	1	2	3	4	5
70	When paperwork cannot be handled right away, I schedule a time to handle it.	1	2	3	4	5
71	We always have an agenda at our meetings - and we stick to it!	1	2	3	4	5
72	We always start our meetings on time.	1	2	3	4	5
73	At our meetings everyone knows clearly what the purpose of the meeting is.	1	2	3	4	5
74	Our meetings end on time.	1	2	3	4	5
75	The leaders at our meetings are chosen because of their ability to run the meeting.	1	2	3	4	5
76	At the end of our meetings, participants are crystal clear on who is to do what.	1	2	3	4	5
77	We ban the use of laptops and cell phones at our meetings.	1	2	3	4	5
78	At our meetings, people speak openly, honestly and respectfully - one at a time.	1	2	3	4	5
79	Our meeting agendas are prepared and distributed 24 hours prior to the meeting.	1	2	3	4	5
80	Following our meetings, a summary of actions to take is distributed to attendees.	1	2	3	4	5
81	I do not work longer hours than my team.	1	2	3	4	5
82	I refrain from giving too much advice when delegating.	1	2	3	4	5
83	I have full confidence in my subordinates to accomplish delegated projects.	1	2	3	4	5

Comprehensive Time-Management Assessment

	SCORING CRITERIA: 1-STRONGLY DISAGREE 2-DISAGREE 3-NEUTRAL 4-AGREE 5-STRONGLY AGREE					
84	If I were to leave my organization today, my department would function just fine.	1	2	3	4	5
85	I rarely work overtime or take work home evenings or weekends.	1	2	3	4	5
86	I do not insist that tasks be done according to the methods I have outlined.	1	2	3	4	5
87	When my staff has completed a task I do not check the details to be sure it's right.	1	2	3	4	5
88	When I return from a vacation there is not a pile of work or emails waiting for me.	1	2	3	4	5
89	I make a real effort to delegate responsibility as well as work to my subordinates.	1	2	3	4	5
90	I am rarely interrupted by my staff asking for information or a decision.	1	2	3	4	5
91	When I look at my appearance, I see what is attractive, not what I'd like to change.	1	2	3	4	5
92	I rarely experience anxiety if I fail to reach the standards I have set for myself.	1	2	3	4	5
93	I am not an perfectonist, nor do I have to win or succeed at everything to be happy.	1	2	3	4	5
94	I am not a neat freak nor am I obsessed with organization.	1	2	3	4	5
95	If I make a mistake at work I do not worry that my boss will view me as incompetent.	1	2	3	4	5
96	I do not have to be in perfect physical shape to be considered attractive.	1	2	3	4	5
97	I am not annoyed that others do not strive, like myself, to do things the right way.	1	2	3	4	5
98	When I delegate a project, I do not expect that it will always be completed perfectly.	1	2	3	4	5
99	My work does not have to be done perfectly for me to be very proud of it.	1	2	3	4	5
100	It didn't bother me that the word "perfectionist" was misspelled in 93 above.	1	2	3	4	5

Comprehensive Time-Management Assessment

SCORING CRITERIA:	1 - STRONGLY DISAGREE 2 - DISAGREE 3 - NEUTRAL 4 - AGREE 5 - STRONGLY AGREE				
101	I never allow people to take advantage of me.	1	2	3	4	5
102	I have no problem saying "no," even to friends and family, and I often do!	1	2	3	4	5
103	I am not a "people pleaser." If people can't accept "no" that's their problem.	1	2	3	4	5
104	I have ways of saying "no" to my boss that work and don't result in hard feelings.	1	2	3	4	5
105	If someone cuts in front of me in a line, I will certainly say something to them.	1	2	3	4	5
106	I do not feel that saying "no" has to have a negative impact on relationships.	1	2	3	4	5
107	I do not feel guilty when I have to say no.	1	2	3	4	5
108	I always make it a habit to set and discuss boundaries with my colleagues at work.	1	2	3	4	5
109	I have no qualms about telling people I do not have the time to do something.	1	2	3	4	5
110	When served something I don't like in a restaurant I will always send it back.	1	2	3	4	5
111	I do not have a problem remembering people's names; one introduction is good.	1	2	3	4	5
112	I rarely forget where I put my glasses or my car or house keys.	1	2	3	4	5
113	I never forget appointments or dates.	1	2	3	4	5
114	I never leave things behind in hotels, planes or rental cars when I am travelling.	1	2	3	4	5
115	I have little difficulty speaking publicly without written notes.	1	2	3	4	5
116	If I am interrupted, I have no trouble regaining my mental momentum.	1	2	3	4	5
117	I have no problem staying focused. My mind doesn't flit from one thing to another.	1	2	3	4	5

Comprehensive Time-Management Assessment

	SCORING CRITERIA: 1 - STRONGLY DISAGREE 2 - DISAGREE 3 - NEUTRAL 4 - AGREE 5 - STRONGLY AGREE					
118	People often remark on how good my memory is.	1	2	3	4	5
119	When concentrating, a loud conversation nearby is not enough to alter my focus.	1	2	3	4	5
120	I seldom come home from the grocery store having forgotten items on my list.	1	2	3	4	5

Interpretation and Analysis

Having now completed the CTMA, please complete the following score sheet in order to identify your relative strengths and weaknesses in each of the 12 areas being measured.

Scoring Instructions:

Beginning on page 30, add together the 10 statements for each of the measurement areas indicated on the score sheet on page 38 and place the sum in the box indicated.

When you have done so for each of the 12 measurement areas, add the sum of all of the measurement areas and place this grand total in the box so labeled at the bottom of the score sheet.

When you have completed the scoring, please turn to page 39, where we will interpret your individual results.

Comprehensive Time-Management Assessment
SCORING

Planning & Prioritization	Question 1 - 10	
Organizing	Question 11 - 20	
Socializing Interruptions	Question 21 - 30	
The Telephone	Question 31 - 40	
Email & Internet	Question 41 - 50	
Procrastination	Question 51 - 60	
Handling Paperwork	Question 61 - 70	
Meetings	Question 71 - 80	
Delegation	Question 81 - 90	
Perfectionism	Question 91 - 100	
Unable to Say "NO"	Question 101 - 110	
Focus and Forgetfulness	Question 111 - 120	

Your Score =

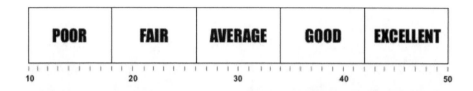

| POOR | FAIR | AVERAGE | GOOD | EXCELLENT |

10   20   30   40   50

| POOR | FAIR | AVERAGE | GOOD | EXCELLENT |

120   240   360   480   600

Evaluation

Examine your score in each of the ten areas of competency being measured on the CTMA.

The ranges are as follows:

Poor	10 - 17
Fair	18 - 25
Average	26 - 30
Very Good	33 - 41
Outstanding	41 - 50

Those areas for which you have scored 20 points or less need work. If your overall score for all 10 evaluated areas falls below 240, you are not at the present time an effective time manager.

Chapter 3

The Time Log

Have you ever driven home after a long and busy day of work thinking to yourself, "What did I really accomplish? It seems like my whole day was a series of interruptions," or, at the end of the week, have you look back and asked yourself, "What did I really do this week? Certainly not those things I set out on Monday to achieve."

If you're like most people, then your answer is yes.

The first step in improving your time management skills is to determine how you're currently spending your time. Keeping a time log is a highly effective way of doing this. You will gain tremendous insight into where your time is actually going. Also, the very act of measuring will raise your awareness of unconscious habits that may be counterproductive. The time log will also help you to identify your time wasters as well as those individuals who interfere most with the accomplishment of your priorities and the realization of your goals.

The first time I kept—or perhaps I should say attempted to keep—a time log was over 30 years ago. At that time, I took the advice being proffered by several time management "experts" and created a form that broke the hours down into 15-minute chunks with a space in which to write what I was doing during each of those allocations of time.

SIMPLE TIME-LOG

TIME	ACTIVITY	CATEGORY	VALUE
8:00 am			
8:15 am			
8:30 am			
8:45 am			
9:00 am			
9:15 am			
9:30 am			
9:45 am			
10:00 am			
10:15 am			
10:30 am			
10:45 am			
11:00 am			
11:15 am			
11:30 am			
11:45 am			
12:00 pm			
12:15 pm			
12:30 pm			
12:45 pm			
1:00 pm			
1:15 pm			
1:30 pm			

But I made every effort to force myself to write down what I was doing every moment of the day, and I found that I was missing a good deal and was failing to record many daily activities as they were occurring, requiring me to go back at the end of the day and "backload" or reconstruct from memory approximating how much time each activity took. This, of course, defeated the purpose of the time log as it essentially reduced its accuracy. Also, the task of recording every minute over a week or two was so daunting that after a few days, I gave up believing that keeping a log was realistic.

I felt bad about my failure from what I perceived to be a lack of self-discipline because I knew that the time log and the information it could provide would be invaluable to helping to identify where my time was going.

It was almost a decade later that I revisited the time log, having discovered a little tool called the Invisible Clock®, a small personal timer that could be set to beep or vibrate at any interval one might choose.

This tool enabled me to resurrect the concept and idea of the time log and I implemented it with much greater success. Now, by creating the timesheet summary similar to that found on page 42, and setting the invisible clock to go off every 15 minutes, I simply had to record what I was doing at that moment when I felt the vibration or heard the beep. While I wasn't recording precisely how much time I was spending on each activity, I discovered that over a period of one or two weeks, it provided essentially the same information.

Now with the advancement of computer apps, there are some great tools available that can effortlessly provide even more accurate information on how you're spending your time. Applications such as

Chrometa® or Qlockwork® simply run in the background on your computer and smartphone and automatically record what you're doing on those devices at a particular moment in time. It records how often and for how long you're writing letters, surfing the Internet, responding to e-mails, etc., as well as providing a simple recording tool for entering the activities in between.

If you never attempted a time log, I would strongly advise you to do so because you almost certainly do not know exactly how you're spending your time or indeed what your time traps and who your time wasters are.

The first time I successfully kept a time log, I was amazed to find that in the over 60 hours that I spent in the office, I only accomplished about 20 hours' worth of real work. This was somewhat disturbing; where did the other 40 hours go?

The log provided the answer: I was checking and reading emails too often, talking on the telephone, doing low-value projects that could have been delegated or didn't need to be done at all, as well as succumbing to all manner of interruptions.

As you might expect, this insight begged some interesting questions. How does my 40% efficacy rate compare with others? If my sense of accomplishment and even my income were dependent on just 20 of the 60 hours I worked, could it be improved, and, if so, how? How could I deal more effectively with the distractions and time wasters taking such a toll on my efficiency?

What I discovered as I studied the subject was that my 40% was very high compared to others and that yes, dramatic improvements could be made that would impact greatly on my sense of accomplishment and income.

Over a period of just a month or two, I was able to almost double my efficiency ratio without increasing my office time. I have also found that this shift has allowed me to increase my effectiveness at work and create a greater sense of balance in all other areas of my life.

I would strongly recommend that you give some serious thought to a personal assessment with the aid of a time log. Choose whatever logging method you wish, but take the time to do it.

Regardless of the method you use to track your time, the importance of the time log comes in the analysis of the data. The activity matrix is shown below. This graphic is meant to describe the four categories in which all of our tasks and activities are found.

The Activity Matrix

IMPORTANT

	YES	NO
YES	1	2
NO	3	4

URGENT

Quadrant 1 is made up of those things that are both important and urgent. These are the things crying out to be done that are obviously of great import. If you fail to accomplish these things, it will be noticed, there will be egg on someone's face – probably yours! These activities also need to be done now. The people and resources are available now but they may not be tomorrow. If these activities or projects are not accomplished now, this will cause a bottleneck and other people, perhaps other members of your team, will not be able to do their work.

Some examples of Quadrant 1 items might be doing the payroll, getting your income tax in on time, or delivering a eulogy. If, God forbid, all three of these things should occur on the same day, they would be accomplished.

Most people do not have difficulty with Quadrant 1 items. Human beings respond to what is urgent, whether it's important not!

This quadrant is the one that causes most of us grief. These are those things in our daily lives that are important but not urgent. I would go further to say that most of the things in our lives that are truly important are not urgent. That change in the relationship you have often thought about, that educational goal, spending more time with your children—these are the most important things in your life but they are not urgent. You can accomplish them tomorrow, or next week, or next month, or sadly, never.

What keeps us from accomplishing Quadrant 2 items? Quadrant 3—items, those things that are not important but urgent. This is the villain in this piece. The villain of urgent and, if you let it, it will grow like a cancer and push everything else out of its way. In Chapter 8, you will learn that the only way to slay this dragon is with the word "NO."

There is a fourth category as well—those things that are neither important nor urgent. You may think, "Why would I ever spend my valuable time doing something that is not important and is not crying out for accomplishment?" The answer comes from the fact that they are fun. They are diversionary. They are much more pleasant than many of the truly important tasks and activities that await us.

The point is that you cannot, absent careful analysis, know accurately how much of your time you are spending on each of these four quadrants. The time log can provide you with invaluable insight in this regard.

Having examined the time logs of scores of individuals over the years, I can tell you that while the results have varied and have often been unique to the individual, there has also been a high degree of commonality when we examine the results in terms of an individual's personality or management style.

It is this role of personality or behavioral style that we examine in the next chapter.

Individual Multidimensional Inventory

On page 87, you will find the Individual Multidimensional Inventory.

The Individual Multidimensional Inventory & Normative Diagnoses (iMind^2) is designed to provide you with an accurate assessment of your individual behavioral style and the relative strengths and weaknesses of that style. More than 50,000 people have taken the Behavioral Styles Profile over the past 35 years. The iMind^2 is both reliable and valid. Statistical reliability assesses the consistency of results across items within a test. The iMind^2 has a high reliability coefficient. Validity refers to the degree to which evidence and theory support the interpretations of the test. There is ample evidence that the application of its tenets has proven highly effective in real-world as well as interpersonal applications.

The iMind^2 has been principally developed from the theories and work of Swiss psychologist Carl Gustav Jung and uniquely combines the latest research in the field of emotional intelligence, including the work of psychologists Howard Gardner of Harvard, Peter Salovey of Yale, as well as John D. Mayer, David R. Caruso, and Daniel Goleman.

Self-awareness, the ability to understand your own behavioral style, is a key factor in effective leadership. A leader is most successful when his or her strongest personal traits are fully engaged. Of equal importance, however, to your leadership ability and personal success is your social awareness—how accurately you can assess the personality and behavioral style of those with whom you must interact. The behavioral styles construct and the iMind^2 can greatly enhance your skills in both of these vital areas.

Having now outlined in some detail the four behavioral styles, it is time to complete the (iMind^2). This instrument will provide you with an accurate self-assessment.

The questions or statements are meant to be mutually exclusive; they are intended to be the opposite of each another.

Chapter 4

Insight and Awareness

I was rereading one of my firm's seminar brochures the other day. The brochure was advertising a working-with-people seminar, and I noticed that throughout the brochure, we spoke time and time again about building trust and rapport in relationships.

It struck me that really these two terms don't necessarily go hand in hand because they're not altogether equal. In order to build true rapport in any relationship, whether in your personal or your professional life, with bosses or with co-workers; with spouses or with children, some level of trust has to exist first.

Many of the failures that we experience in our relationships stem from the fact that there's a lack of trust in those relationships.

The research teaches us that in order for trust to exist in any relationship, three conditions first must be present. In all trusting relationships, we find as a feature of those relationships contingency. In order to experience trust in those relationships, there must be contingency; that is, the person to whom we give our trust must at least be perceived by us as being in a position to affect us or influence our behavior in some important or significant way. Without contingency, there's no opportunity for trust to exist and probably no reason for it to exist.

Secondly, in all trusting relationships, we find as a feature of those relationships the principle of predictability. In order to have trust, we must have some level of confidence in expectations as to the behavior of the trusted person. You can't have trust without predictability. You can have hope. If I'm walking down one of the backstreets of Chicago late at night with a large amount of money in my pocket and I hear noises ahead in the shadows, I may hope that it's a policeman, but that's not the same thing as trusting that it is a policeman.

Finally, in all trusting relationships, we find as a feature of those relationships alternative options, or free will. We all have free will, and for trust to exist, we have to be able to exercise it freely. In other words, you can't compel people to trust you; people have to exercise their free will in a relationship in order for trust to exist.

Now, I know that this is probably as clear as mud, but let me give you an example that may bring some clarity to the role of these three features.

Consider the good farmer who is working on repairing a damaged piece of equipment, let's say a pump at the bottom of a shallow well. His labors take him a period of six or seven hours, and his wife, recognizing the fact that her husband won't be returning for lunch, which is his custom, says to their daughter Susan, "Suzy, would you take this bagged lunch to Daddy at the well site?"

Well, the obedient daughter does as she's told, but when she appears at the site of the well, she can't see her father anywhere, she calls out, "Daddy?"

She hears from the depths of the well, "I'm down here, Suzy."

Suzy walks to the edge of the dark pit and looks down, but all she can see below is the darkness of the well, she calls again, "Daddy?"

Her father responds, "Yes, Suzy, I'm down here, what can I do for you?"

Suzy answers, "I have brought you your lunch!"

Her father shouts back, "Suzy, I've got some grease on my hands. Just toss it in."

Suzy again responds, "But I can't see you!"

Her father shouts back, "I know it's dark down here, but I can see you. Just toss it in."

Suzy walks to the edge of the pit and throws it in, and she can hear her father catch it.

But then her father shouts back, "Suzy, why don't you join me for lunch? Just jump in and I'll catch you." Suzy again looks down the well, but all she can see is the blackness of the hole; however, trusting in the relationship that she has with her father, she leaps into the darkness, and of course, her father catches her.

Then let me ask you this question: What was the contingency in that relationship? Was the father, the trusted person in this instance, in a position to affect his daughter in some important or significant way? Yes. Had the father been negligent in his responsibility or duty to catch his daughter, the child could have been seriously injured. Yes, there was contingency.

Was there predictability? Was the trusting person, in this case Suzy, able to predict her father's behavior in this instance? Yes. Again, had it been a hired hand or other stranger, would she have been as likely to jump?

Finally, were there alternative options available to Suzy? Was she compelled to leap into the darkness? No. Suzy could have done many other things. She could have said, "No, that's fine. I'll walk down the ladder." She could have said, "No, I'll just sit on the edge and talk to you." Or she could have run home to Mother. There were all kinds of alternatives available to Suzy.

The problem with the concept of trust is that, like many other things we will examine here, what works for one person will not always or necessarily work for another.

If you read history or if you read philosophy, consider that there has long been recognition that human beings are uniquely and individually different. We really are like snowflakes; no two of us are exactly alike.

Often at my public seminars, I will flash faces on the screen of well known but controversial characters such as George W. Bush, President Barack Obama, Donald Trump, Nancy Grace, or Jimmy Swaggart, then I will ask people to write down the first word that comes to their mind when they see these faces flashed on the screen. The result is that there is a wide range of responses from very positive to extremely negative. In fact, I've yet to find one person that everyone unanimously responds to either favorably or unfavorably.

Why do some people see George W. Bush as the Savior of the Western world while others seem to see him as the devil incarnate? Why is it in the United States approximately half the people vote Republican and the other half Democrat?

The fact is that just as some people have different physical characteristics, such as height or weight or gender, so too do they differ in the way that they see things, the way they interpret the world around them, and react to it, as well as a way that they relate to other people.

But there is another message to learn from history and philosophy, and that is that while people may be uniquely and individually different, they also tend to fall into types.

The great physician and philosopher Hippocrates recognized this fact. He spoke about the four temperaments of man: the phlegmatic, sanguine, melancholic, and choleric. He found from his experience that all the people he interacted with tended to fall into one of these four types.

In the tenth and eleventh centuries, the Sufis (a mystical sect of Islam) spoke of the Enneagram, a model that identified three essential types or triads (feelers and relaters and doers) with three personality sub-styles within each.

But the dividing of the human family into distinct types isn't some vague proposition lost in antiquity, somehow attached to the occult and indicative of arcane thinking.

Some of the greatest psychologists of all time, Carl Gustav Jung[12] in particular - have been drawn to the same conclusion. Jung spent a lifetime observing, researching, and analyzing personality, and at the end of his life and career, he suggested that there were four general archetypes or personalities. Jung used different words than Hippocrates to describe his four types; he speaks of sensates, intuitives, feelers, and rational thinkers, but in many ways he was saying the same thing.

Back in the 1970s, another model became very popular in the business community called the "management grid[13]." The research behind the management grid came from Ohio State University[14] and the work they did in their business faculty and school in the 1960s. This model was picked up by a couple of writers and consultants by the name of Blake and Mouton, who popularized this model and found ingenious ways to apply it to almost every occupational group in society.

From the graphic below, we can see that there are two key parameters that the model is concerned with measuring. On the X-axis we have task orientation, and on the Y-axis we have consideration.

The Management Grid
Blake & Mouton

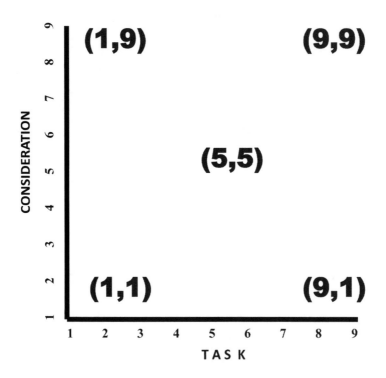

This model suggests that all of us - all people in the workplace are concerned with two key parameters: task and consideration. But we're not all the same; some of us are extremely high or extremely low or in the middle on both. The "management grid" emerges through the unique combination of these two parameters.

The authors would suggest that each one of us is concerned, to a greater or lesser degree in the workplace, with getting the job done. Some of us are extremely task-oriented; we take the perspective of, "I have a job to do, don't get in my way!" Others are less concerned with task, recognizing that other things are equally important. And some people seem to lack task orientation altogether. They take the perspective that, "If we get this job done today, that's great, if we don't get to it today and do it tomorrow, that's great, and if we don't get to it at all, that's fine as well!"

On the consideration scale, some people are extremely high, very much concerned with the needs and feelings of other people, while other people at the same time seem to lack consideration.

Those towards the top of the consideration scale bend over backwards to accommodate other people. If that other person is hurting, they are hurting. They go out of their way to avoid a scene.

While those in the middle are politically more astute and concerned with the needs and feelings of other people, they view other factors as being of equal importance.

Finally, those people scoring towards the bottom of the consideration scale rarely consider the needs of other people. They make no pretense, and they are never accused of being politically correct. They tell people what they think and let the chips fall where they may.

It is through this unique combination of task and consideration that this matrix-like model emerges. The model suggests that if you can identify where the key actors in your life fall, in terms of their unique combination of task and consideration, then you can explain their behavior and, more importantly, can predict their behavior.

I believe that this is why people find models of this ilk so interesting; they allow us to predict how others will respond to our actions.

Would it not be beneficial to understand how your customers will respond to the offer you wish to advertise before you take the time and spend the money to do so? Would it not be useful to understand how your boss will typically respond to your actions before you take those actions? Would it not be beneficial to be able to understand how your spouse will respond to changes you hope to make in your relationship before you make them?

My own feeling is that the management grid is great as far as it goes, but I think it fails to take into consideration a couple of very important parameters in human personality and management style.

For one thing, the model doesn't speak to the role of assertiveness in the choices made available to you. Were you born or socialized to respond assertively with those around you? I think this is a key characteristic or defining feature of personality. I think this key element must be integrated into any useful or accurate model of personality or management style.

Secondly, the model doesn't speak to the role of emotional responsiveness or emotional expressiveness as a determinant of personality.

The model I am about to present to you, the Behavioral Styles Model, is the best model available for accurate self-assessment, and I feel it also provides the greatest opportunity through its application to enrich the experiences we have with others by developing stronger relationships with them.

The Behavioral Styles Model

Think of a line drawn across a page. At one side of the line (the right side) is written the word "assertive." At the end of the line (the left side) is written the word "non-assertive."

The assertive end of the line indicates a person who is totally assertive in all relationships, at all times, under all circumstances. Clearly, no one would be at this end of the line, the ideal example of assertiveness. Many of us are very assertive individuals, but we're not the ideal example of assertiveness. Nor is there anyone totally at the left end of the continuum, totally lacking any assertive abilities, totally passive, never defends his or her rights, and has the word "victim" stenciled across their forehead. Some of us are non-assertive, particularly in certain social situations, but we're not the ideal example of non-assertiveness.

Now, before we can determine where we fall on this continuum, we have to come up with a definition of what "assertiveness" is. When I ask people at my seminars to define the word "assertive," they typically describe the behaviors of assertive people, and while this approach is useful and altogether appropriate, it's not the same as the definition.

The two key components or parameters of the Behavioral Styles Model are assertiveness and emotional responsiveness.

Assertiveness

If you were to take your pen and draw a horizontal line across a sheet of paper, label the right end of the line "assertiveness" and the left end "non-assertiveness," we would all be found somewhere along this line.

Some of us, by our own nature it would seem, are assertive, and some of us have been educated or socialized to behave assertively. These people would be found on the right-hand side of the line. Others, by their nature (and for reasons we'll delve into later), behave non-assertively or passively in their interactions with other people. These people would be found on the left-hand side of the line.

But what is assertiveness? How can it be defined? When I ask this question at public seminars, the typical responses are the ability to voice one's concern, appearing confident, the ability to say "no" when appropriate, or the ability to take initiative, etc.

I usually point out to the group at this point that what they've given me is not a definition of "assertiveness," but rather they have described the behaviors of assertive people.

We can take one of two perspectives as we try to come to an understanding of human behavior.

We can take a purely psychological approach, in which we try to burrow into the minds of other people and determine what their motivations were, what their intent was. I think this path is very dangerous, to play psychoanalyst. Alternatively, we can take a behavioral approach, the approach most people instinctively take, and speak to observable, notable behaviors.

Below is a list of common, but notable, observable behaviors of assertive people. As we go through this list, think about how many of these characteristics, and to what degree and extent, are representative of your normal behaviors.

Assertive Indicators

Firm Handshake	Strong Opinions
Fast-Paced	Leans into Conversations
Direct Eye Contact	Initiator of Conversations
Risk-Taking	Confrontational
Voice Intonation	Confidence
Decisiveness	Powerful First Impression

Let me elaborate a little on each of these behavioral features:

1. Handshake

    When an assertive individual meets another person, they
    grab hold, they squeeze, and they shake, whereas when a
    non-assertive person meets another hand, which is usually
    extended only in response to the other's initiation, it is more
    likely to be a touch or light acceptance of the other grip.
    Now, obviously this is not conclusive or solely indicative of
    assertive or non-assertive behaviors. Many of us are taught
    as children that we should always have a firm handshake, but
    there is nonetheless a correlation between a firm handshake
    and an assertive personality.

2. Pace

    There is a higher correlation between pace and assertiveness.
    Generally speaking, assertive people are high-energy, fast-
    paced individuals. They move quickly from one activity to
    another. There is animation and motion. The non-assertive
    person, on the other hand, appears more cautious, with
    smaller movements, and appears slower in action and
    behavior.

3. Direct Eye Contact

    Clearly, there is a higher level of direct eye contact in the
    case of the assertive person. When communicating with
    another, they look that person in the eye, whereas with the
    non-assertive person, the focus is indirect; they look around
    at other people, and they simply are more likely to make eye
    contact more intermittently and, at the extreme, may look
    away.

4. Risk-Taking

    The assertive person takes greater risks, which is observed in
    terms of their communicating behaviors which are wide
    ranging and include vocal intonation and modulation; they
    use their bodies to communicate; they gesture; they move
    around. The non-assertive person tends to be more static;
    they speak more slowly and softly and may even speak in
    monotone. They tend not to gesture or use their bodies to
    the same degree as the assertive person.

5. Decisiveness

    The assertive person is more readily able to make quick
    decisions; they are not always good, but they are quick! The
    non-assertive person labors over even the most
    inconsequential decisions. They tend to be more cautious
    and careful.

6. Strong Opinions

    The assertive individual tends to express strong opinions vs.
    mild, tenuous statements. "This is my opinion; this is what I
    think; this is the truth." The non-assertive person, on the
    other hand, tends to say things like, "Don't you think
    that..."or, "Maybe, couldn't it possibly be...."

7. Initiation of Conversation

    The assertive person is more likely to initiate the
    conversation. The non-assertive person is more likely to
    defer. "I'm not going to say something until he says
    something."

8. Confident Appearance

The assertive person appears confident rather than shy; they confront rather than go along.

Generally speaking, we see the assertive person as powerful and the non-assertive person as friendly or nice.

Look again at the list above. According to these characteristics or this set of criteria, in terms of assertiveness, are you left of center or right of center?

Later in this chapter, I will be asking you to take the Individual Multidimensional Inventory (iMind^2) that will allow you to accurately determine where you fall on the assertiveness scale, but before we go there, let's complete our model.

Emotional Responsiveness

If you were to take your pen and draw a vertical line bisecting the assertiveness line in the center and label the top of this line "expressiveness" and the bottom of this line "non-expressiveness," everyone could again be found on that line.

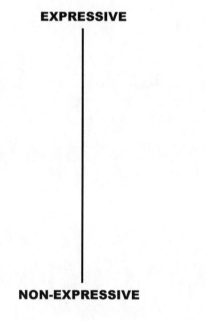

EXPRESSIVE

NON-EXPRESSIVE

Some of us, those of us scoring toward the top of this line, are very much people-oriented. We need to work with and around others; we are good team players; we dislike being alone. Others, on the other hand, would rather work individually on projects; we would rather spend our time individually solving problems than attending meetings or seeking consensus with others.

Below are some of the behavioral characteristics of expressive and non-expressive people:

Expressiveness

Animated Facial Expression	**Personable and Open**
Use of Gestures	**Less Use of Time**
Playfulness	**Informal Dress Code**
Comfortable with Small Talk	**Shows Feelings**
Decisions Based on Feelings	**Seeks Contact**
Personal Manner of Supervision	**Feelings-Oriented**

A little explanation is also required here:

1. Animated Facial Expression

    It is not that difficult to identify an Expressive because their emotions radiate in their countenance. When they're happy, they laugh; when they're sad, it shows; and when someone hurts their feelings, they may say it doesn't matter, but it matters. On the other hand, the Non-Expressive, they may not be stoic, but they are clearly less animated than the Expressive.

2. The Use of Gestures

   Expressives tend to use their bodies to communicate. They
   gesture; they move around. Non-Expressives, in contrast,
   tend to be more static. Their movements are small and
   controlled.

3. Playfulness

   Expressives appear more playful; Non-Expressives more
   serious. Non-Expressives are suspicious of those who use
   humor, particularly in situations where they feel it is
   inappropriate.

4. Dress Codes

   Although far from conclusive, dress codes can also be an
   indicator of expressiveness. If an Expressive is not sure what
   appropriate dress is for a given occasion, they will generally
   suit themselves. If anything, they will err in the direction of
   informality. In the case of the Non-Expressive, if they are
   not sure what dress is appropriate, they will typically
   overdress, moving in the direction of formality.

5. Feelings Orientation

The Expressive also tends to show their feelings, whereas the Non-Expressive tends to hide their feelings. I'm not suggesting that Expressives feel and Non-Expressives don't feel. We are all human beings; we all feel. But in the expression of emotion is a grave difference, and it is partly a function of behavioral style.

6. Small Talk

Expressives are more comfortable with small talk, with what I call "drapery talk," the kind of meaningless conversational claptrap that acts as a social lubricant. "I like your drapes." "Warm day but humid." "Did you see the football game last night?" Whereas Non-Expressives find it difficult to engage in this type of conversational drivel. They think to themselves, "I've nothing in common with this woman, what am I going to talk about, the weather, the football game, those ugly drapes!"

7. Decision-Making

Expressives often make decisions based on, and motivated by, their feelings. They may say things like, "I just don't feel right about what went on," or, "My wee small voice is shouting at me," or, "My intuition tells me such-and-such." Non-Expressives are more likely to say things like, "I don't think this is the right course of action," or, "The facts don't indicate such-and-such," or, "The data isn't friendly."

8. Personable and Open

   Expressives appear to be more personable and open to others. Non-Expressives appear more closed and aloof.

9. The Use of Time

   In terms of the use of time, there is a significant difference between Expressives and Non-Expressives. Expressives are more flexible as they approach projects and assignments, being able to reprioritize when necessary. Non-Expressives, on the other hand, become stressed when changing conditions disrupts their plans.

10. Supervision

   In the case of the Expressive, supervision is often done in a personal manner. If they think it might help improve a given situation, they won't hesitate to go out for a drink or out to dinner with the staff to discuss a situation or problem. Not so with the Non-Expressive. They believe in maintaining a "professional distance." They say to themselves, "I'm not going to take them out for a drink. They might start to like me!" These are the people who say, "It's not wise for doctors and nurses to fraternize." "It's not wise for officers and enlisted men to drink together." "It's unwise for management and labor to come together. It's an adversarial world we live in, and people have to know their place."

In essence, Expressives seek contact, emotional contact, with other people. Non-Expressives, on the other hand, are seeking to avoid contact. Expressives are feelings-oriented. Non-Expressives are thinking-oriented.

It's through the unique combination of these two parameters that the Behavioral Styles Model emerges. The model suggests that there are four distinct social or behavioral styles.

Some people are highly assertive and highly expressive; these individuals we will label as Dreamers. In the general population in the United States, they account for approximately 27%.

Some people share the emotional responsiveness of the Dreamer but are less than average when it comes to assertiveness. These individuals, accounting for 25% of the population, we will call Supporters.

Some 23% of the population are assertive and at the same time non-expressive and task-oriented. We will label these people with the title Commander.

Finally, approximately 24% of the population is both non-assertive and non-expressive. We will refer to these as Thinkers.

The Behavioral Styles Profile

The Behavioral Styles Model is both a very simple tool (describing four basic styles), as well as a fairly complex tool, allowing for the fact that no two people are exactly the same.

And herein lies one of its main differentiators from many of the other more common personality profiling tools. Not only will you fall generally within one particular behavioral style, but the model also accepts that you may display different behavioral responses in your various relationships, as well, you will have shades of all four behavioral styles within your make-up, resulting in your inclusion in one of sixteen sub-types or temperaments. So two people of the same basic behavioral style can and do act quite differently.

Behavioral Style Profile

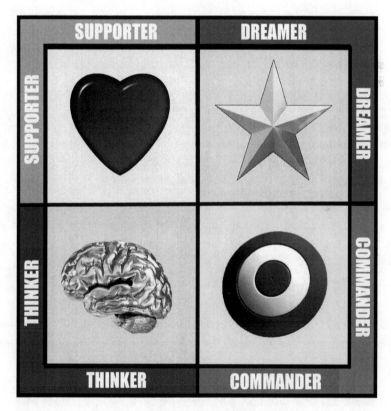

Color Plate on Page 235

There are some of us who are highly assertive individuals but who also like to work with and around other people. We're going to call these individuals "Dreamers." The term is somewhat pejorative, but I will explain in due course why I chose the word "Dreamer" to describe this combination – assertiveness and emotional responsiveness, or expressiveness.

There are some of us who are highly assertive but more task- than people-oriented. These people, while wanting to maintain good relationships with others, will, in a pinch, choose the accomplishment of an important task over the approval of other people. They are assertive and task-oriented. We'll call these people "Commanders."

Some people enjoy social interaction with others very much. They are good team players and work well with other people; however, in terms of assertiveness, they're below average. They will choose relationship success over other types of accomplishments in their lives. These individuals we're going to refer to with the title "Supporter."

And there are some people who are neither highly assertive nor are they people-oriented. They are concerned more with tasks and their accomplishments and are at the same time non-assertive. These individuals we will refer to as "Thinkers."

Before we delve even further into this model, I would suggest to you that the most toxic relationships we could find ourselves in are the diagonals in this model. For example, there is considerable interpersonal stress when Commanders and Supporters try to work together. They have absolutely nothing in common.

Supporters are filled with the milk of human kindness; they are supportive and encouraging to others, they go out of their way to avoid a scene, sometimes giving in even when they know they are right rather than have conflict enter the relationship. They are aware of and concerned with the needs and feelings of other people. They want everyone to experience high levels of self-esteem. The Commander, on the other hand, takes the, "Damn the torpedoes! Full speed ahead!" approach. They are much more concerned with accomplishment than with relationships.

Likewise, there's a tendency towards conflict or certainly a social uneasiness when Dreamers and Thinkers seek to communicate for the purposes of accomplishing a task or project. The Dreamer manages by the seat of their pants. They possess the "gift of the gab"; that is, the ability to speak with all types of people. While they tend to be effective motivators, they are not detail-oriented and can sometimes be perceived as flighty by other people. It is for this reason that they tend to have difficulty communicating and working effectively with the task-oriented Thinker.

Now, clearly we have conflicts with the people next door, the style adjacent to our own. Dreamers and Supporters have conflicts, as do Commanders and Thinkers; Supporters and Thinkers, as do Dreamers and Commanders, but they are never as great as these diagonals. The reason for this is that in the case of the diagonals, there is no commonality. Dreamers and Supporters are both people-oriented, and they make decisions accordingly. The source of their conflict stems from the fact that one (the Dreamer) will control the relationship.

Dreamers and Commanders have assertiveness in common. One will not dominate the other; the conflict comes from differing priorities. The Dreamer's priority is people and relationships, whereas the Commander's priority is task.

Commanders and Thinkers are both task-oriented individuals concerned less with social interaction and the interpersonal niceties than they are with accomplishing the goal or task in both an effective and efficient manner. Over time, the Commander will usually move to dominate decision-making, resulting in hard feelings.

And while Supporters and Thinkers have non-assertiveness in common (meaning one will not dominate the other), their priorities again are really quite different. The Supporter's priority is the maintenance of relationships with others, while the Thinker's priority is problem-solving and goal attainment.

You may have recognized through this discussion that you tend to fall closer to one of these four behavioral styles than the others.

One point I would like you to understand, however, is that we all have elements of each of the four styles within our personality. One is simply more predominant. It is for this reason that our personality seems to differ from one relationship to the next.

The Behavioral Styles Matrix below indicates the relationships between the two parameters expressiveness and assertiveness.

Behavioral Styles Matrix

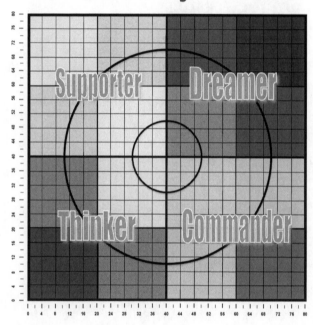

On the next few pages, we will examine the four styles in some detail.

Style Characteristics
The DREAMER

1. Spontaneous

2. Outgoing, Fun-loving

3. Enthusiastic

4. Generalizes – Not Detail-Oriented

5. Exaggerates

6. Seeks Involvement

7. Dislikes Being Alone

8. Works Quickly – High Energy

9. Anecdotal

10. Seeks Self-Esteem and a Sense of Belonging

The Dreamer is spontaneous. They often leap before they look. They have a bias for action. Not big on research or homework, they manage by the seat of their pants. They are responsive and sometimes reactionary.

They are outgoing, fun loving, and enthusiastic. The life of the party, they have the "gift of the gab," the ability to speak with anyone about anything.

This ability to put other people at ease draws others in, encouraging them to communicate, another facility the Dreamer has is their ability to lead others to higher levels of motivation.

Some may, however, perceive them as coming on too strong, monopolizing the conversation, or being too brash.

The greatest single feature of their personality is their enthusiasm. Their enthusiasm is contagious. They can dream and get other people caught up in that dream. That is why I chose the moniker Dreamer to label them.

They are so passionate about their dream, idea, or commitment that they can lead others to share their dream to come on side, to agree with them or vote for them or to sign on the dotted line.

However, they tend to generalize too much, and they are not detail-oriented. They become easily bored, and when they do become bored, they will often jump too quickly from one activity to the next, leaving some tasks undone. They also tend to exaggerate.

The Dreamer seeks involvement with other people. They dislike being alone. They hate budget time, when they are forced to retreat to their own offices for two or three weeks of work on the budget. They will find any excuse to get out of their office and interrupt other people. They simply cannot work on their own for long periods of time without any interaction with other people.

They are anecdotal in their communications and interesting people to be around. They use colorful, expressive language, illustrating points with stories, examples, or parables. They usually have a great sense of humor.

What they really seek is self-esteem and a sense of belonging; what Abraham Maslow[13] called the "ego needs" and "social needs." They want to feel part of a group, but they also want to be recognized; they want to be stroked. They want others to know that they are superior in some way than the group norm.

If we were to pencil in their greatest single skill, we might use the word "persuasiveness." The Dreamer can persuade others to action; they motivate other people to act. This is a powerful skill in organizational life. The ability to share one's vision with others is a key component of leadership.

Their intent is to get appreciation or applause. The symbol might be the star. They want the center stage; they want other people to recognize their talents and their value.

A few examples of Dreamers from popular culture might be comedic actors Jim Carrey and Robin Williams, or comedienne Ellen DeGeneres. Many talk-show hosts come from this quadrant, David Letterman, Jay Leno, Conan O'Brien, and Craig Ferguson are examples. The Dreamer's quick wit and sense of humor make them ideally suited to the world of entertainment.

Sales, marketing, or advertising are other occupations that Dreamers are drawn to. Have you known salespeople imbued with all the strengths of the Dreamer, the ability to motivate other people to action, who can get prospects emotionally involved in the purchase of their good or service?

Perhaps you have also known salespeople guilty of the weaknesses of the Dreamer, who lack detail, who become easily bored - the salesperson that tends to lose their enthusiasm once the sale has been made or fails to follow through on promises made before you signed on the dotted line.

Politics, at least the old-style baby kissing, backslapping, glad-handing politician.

We find accountants coming from this quadrant, as well as engineers, CEOs, and human resource specialists, but we find a predominance of people coming from the world of entertainment, advertising, politics, and sales.

Style Characteristics
The SUPPORTER

1. Cooperative

2. Slow in Action and Decisions

3. Dislikes and Avoids Conflict

4. Seeks Close Personal Relationships

5. Patient, Diplomatic, Loyal, and Dependable

6. Highly Supportive of Others

7. Weak at Goal-Setting and Self-Direction

8. Seeks Security and a Sense of Belonging

The Supporter is more cooperative than the Dreamer. Dreamers need recognition; they need others to recognize their status and uniqueness. Supporters, on the other hand, do not have this kind of ego involvement and therefore tend to be much more cooperative. It does not matter as much to the Supporter that others recognize that their contribution was greater than the contribution of their colleagues. They take the perspective, "As long as we succeed, as long as the team thrives, as long as the organization grows, I'm happy." This focus on "we" rather than "I" leads to a greater level of cooperation.

Supporters tend to be slow in action and decisions, however. Unlike the Dreamer, who is tearing at the bit, with a bias for action, who leaps before looking, the Supporter focuses more on relationships. Rather than moving too quickly to action, they take a sober second thought, ensuring that their actions will not in any way erode their relationships.

Another defining feature of their style is their tendency to avoid conflict wherever possible. They believe that conflict is something that needs to be avoided, not worked through. This causes them endless problems. They find it difficult to say "no," even when others are blatantly taking advantage of them. By avoiding confrontation, pressure spots emerge and remain.

They seek close personal relationships with other people. They don't need a lot of friends, but they need a few good, close friends. Often the relationships they make in high school they maintain for a lifetime. They go to reunions and will stay in touch.

They are patient, diplomatic, loyal, and dependable. They make good friends because they are great listeners. They are always in your corner. This has great utility in modern organizations because it encourages others toward completion.

Their greatest weakness comes from their greatest strength. They are so concerned with helping others accomplish their goals and service their needs, that too often they neglect their own needs and wants. This can lead to unhappiness in their lives, coming to the realization that they take care of everyone else's needs, but no one takes care of their needs.

Their needs are security and a sense of belonging, what Abraham Maslow, in his hierarchy of needs, called the "social" and the "safety needs." They choose safe careers and safe relationships.

Their single greatest skill is listening.

Their intent is to get along, and their symbol might be the heart. They are lovers; they are certainly not fighters. They're drawn to occupations where listening is essential, psychologist, counselor, diagnostic physician, priest.

Some examples of Supporters might be Mahatma Gandhi, Princess Diana, Jimmy Carter, Walter Cronkite, or Katie Couric

Style Characteristics
The THINKER

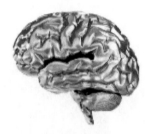

1. Cautious in Actions and Decisions

2. Seeks Organization and Structure

3. Logical and Systematic

4. Dislikes Involvement with People

5. Prefers Objective, Task-Oriented Work

6. Fact-Oriented Questioning

7. Seeks Security and Self-Actualization

In the lower left-hand quadrant, we have the Thinker.

The Thinker is cautious in actions and decisions. They have to know the rules of the game before they are willing to play. They seek organization and structure - they demand it.

They are fact-oriented and ask a lot of questions, and they seek a lot of data before they feel comfortable moving forward.

They are logical and systematic people. When they do a job, they do it right, the scientific method. They determine and establish all the alternatives, they evaluate each of those alternatives, and then they choose the most critical path to the attainment of the optimal alternative or solution.

Sometimes, however, they are so focused on efficiency that they lose track of effectiveness.

They dislike involvement with people. Simply stated, their single greatest weakness is their inability to work effectively with other human beings.

They prefer objective, task-oriented, intellectual work.

Their greatest skill is their ability to solve problems. They are tenacious in seeking out the best solution. You might give them a problem and forget that you have given them a problem, but they don't forget, they don't get bored, or jump to a less-challenging task; they will hang in until they come up with a solution.

The Thinker's determination to get it right makes them essential to organizational success.

They are drawn to occupations that afford them the opportunity to solve problems and accomplish tasks individually, without major group interaction. Accounting, engineering, and the pure sciences fit well.

Stereotypical examples of Thinkers might be Albert Einstein, Woody Allen, or Bill Gates.

Style Characteristics
The COMMANDER

1. Strong and Independent

2. Firm in Actions and Decisions

3. Seeks Control

4. Pragmatic and Efficient

5. Low Tolerance for the Feelings of Others

6. Works Quickly, Decisively, Impressively - ALONE

7. Seeks Self-Esteem and Self-Realization

The final behavioral style is the Commander. They are highly assertive and non-expressive.

They are strong and independent individuals, firm in action and decisions. When they set a goal, it is hard to dissuade them from the accomplishment of that goal.

Not only do they seek control, they demand it.

They are pragmatic and efficient people, and for them, the end often justifies the means. This leads, at times, to their single greatest weakness, a low tolerance for the needs and feelings of others.

This weakness can erode their overall success and effectiveness.

There greatest skill is their administrative skill, because one of the key functions of management and administration is coordination, and they are good at that. They can make the difficult decisions often required in key organizational positions in a measured, rational, non-emotional way. Their intent is to get it done.

The story goes that Lee Iacocca, who has been credited with Chrysler, used to have a sign on his desk that read "Just Do It!"

Commanders often choose occupations and careers that provide them with power and control - law, medicine, and of course, the military (from which I chose their moniker). Not always successful in middle-management roles, they come into their own in the executive suite. Many entrepreneurs score out to be Commanders.

Some examples of Commanders from popular culture would be Donald Trump, George W. Bush, Jack Kennedy, Adolph Hitler, and Simon Cowell.

Individual Multidimensional Inventory

On page 87 you will find the Individual Multidimensional Inventory.

The Individual Multidimensional Inventory & Normative Diagnoses (iMind^2) is designed to provide you with an accurate assessment of your individual behavioral style and the relative strengths and weaknesses of that style. More than 50,000 people have taken the Behavioral Styles Profile over the past 35 years, the iMind^2 is both reliable and valid. Statistical reliability assesses the consistency of results across items within a test. The iMind^2 has a high reliability coefficient. Validity refers to the degree to which evidence and theory support the interpretations of the test. There is ample

---

evidence that the application of its tenets has proven highly effective in real-world applications as well as interpersonal.

The iMind^2 has been principally developed from the theories and work of the Swiss psychologist Carl Gustav Jung and uniquely combines the latest research in the field of emotional intelligence, including the work of psychologists Howard Gardner of Harvard, Peter Salovey of Yale, as well as John D. Mayer, David R. Caruso, and Daniel Goleman.

Self-awareness, the ability to understand your own behavioral style, is a key factor in effective leadership. A leader is most successful when his or her strongest personal traits are fully engaged. Of equal importance, however, to your leadership ability and personal success is your social awareness; how accurately you can assess the personality and behavioral style of those with whom you must interact. The behavioral styles construct and the iMind^2 can greatly enhance your skills in both of these vital areas.

Having now outlined in some detail the four behavioral styles, it is time to complete the Individual Multidimensional Inventory & Normative Diagnoses (iMind^2). This instrument will provide you with an accurate self-assessment.

The questions or statements are meant to be mutually exclusive; they are intended to be the opposite of one another.

Chapter 5

The Individual Multidimensional Inventory & Diagnoses (iMind²)

Instructions:

For the following pages, you will find 100 bipolar statements. Please read each pair carefully, and then circle the number CLOSEST to the statement that best describes your behavior or belief. For example, if you feel the statement on the left more accurately describes your behavior or belief than the statement on the right, you should circle the zero. If, on the other hand, you feel that the statement on the right is more reflective of your behavior or belief than the statement on the left, you should circle the number two. Circle the number one if (and only if) you feel that neither statement is even slightly more reflective of your behavior or belief, that is, you agree with both statements equally.

For the first 50 statements, please respond in terms of your <u>work relationships only</u>; that is, think only of your interactions with bosses, co-workers, subordinates, clients, customers, suppliers, etc. For the second set of 50 bipolar statements, please read both statements carefully, then circle the number CLOSEST to the statement that best describes your behavior or belief. <u>Please respond in terms of your personal or non-work relationships only</u>; that is, think only of your interactions with your partner, friends, family, neighbors, waiters, shop clerks, etc.

iMind² Behavioral Styles Assessment

#	(0) I agree MORE with the Statement on the Left	(1) I agree with both EQUILY			(2) I agree MORE with the Statement on the Right
1	I would rather work individually on a project than work as a member of a team.	0	1	2	I would rather work as a member of a team than work alone.
2	I rarely socialize with the people I work with.	0	1	2	I often socialize with the people I work with.
3	I am not a very intuitive person; I go with what people say - not with what they don't say!	0	1	2	I am a very intuitive person; I can often "read between the lines" to identify what the real message is.
4	My co-workers would probably say I am more task-oriented than people-oriented.	0	1	2	My co-workers would probably say I am more people-oriented than task-oriented.
5	I can't say I am really in touch with my co-workers' and subordinates' feelings.	0	1	2	I am very much in touch with my co-workers' and subordinates' feelings.
6	I am project driven and think it is more important to be successful than be well-liked.	0	1	2	I am not driven; to me it is more important to have superior work relationships than personal success.
7	I am methodical and systematic preferring structure and familiar routines.	0	1	2	I am intuitive, creative and sometimes impulsive. I dislike routine.
8	I am thinking-oriented.	0	1	2	I am feelings-oriented.
9	I am cautious in the decisions I make at work; I do not like to take risks and seldom do.	0	1	2	I believe to achieve success, one must take chances and I take calculated risks when appropriate.
10	Accomplishing the task and getting the job done is more important to me than being well liked.	0	1	2	Being well liked is as important to me as accomplishing a goal or task at work.

iMind² Behavioral Styles Assessment

#	(0) I agree MORE with the Statement on the Left	(1) I agree with both EQUILY			(2) I agree MORE with the Statement on the Right
11	I believe that emotions should be always governed by reason.	0	1	2	Letting someone else witness my emotions does not bother me.
12	I view working with other people as a necessary evil.	0	1	2	Relationships are the most important thing; it's what life is all about.
13	When correcting someone's errors at work, I don't worry about jeopardizing the relationship.	0	1	2	When correcting mistakes at work, I seek to find a way that will not jeopardize my relationships.
14	When I come to work in the morning, I start by organizing my tasks and activities.	0	1	2	When I come to work in the morning, I usually start by socializing with my co-workers.
15	I don't like interpersonal conflict at work and probably don't handle it all that well.	0	1	2	Nobody likes conflict, but I think my interpersonal skills help me to deal with it effectively.
16	To be honest, I don't encourage my team to participate in decision-making.	0	1	2	I honestly encourage my team to participate in decision-making.
17	I show very little facial expression when communicating with my co-workers.	0	1	2	I show a good deal of facial expression when communicating with my co-workers.
18	I focus heavily on accomplishment and achievement, often putting it ahead of relationships.	0	1	2	I generally put my relationships and teamwork ahead of individual accomplishment and achievement.
19	I don't enjoy office parties, picnics or other social functions with the people I work with.	0	1	2	I really like to get together socially with the people I work with.
20	I can work patiently on a project until it is completed. My problem-solving skill is one of my greatest strengths.	0	1	2	I need to work with people; I get a little "antsy" when I have to work too long on a single project alone.

iMind^2 Behavioral Styles Assessment

#	(0) I agree MORE with the Statement on the Left	(1) I agree with both EQUILY			(2) I agree MORE with the Statement on the Right
21	I am not really in touch with my co-workers' feelings.	0	1	2	I am very much in touch with my co-workers' feelings.
22	I am logical and rational.	0	1	2	I am imaginative and creative.
23	My communication is usually direct, down to earth and focused on the task at hand.	0	1	2	My communication at work is somewhat indirect and abstract; focused on our overall mission.
24	I model independent qualities such as determination, problem-solving, personal effort and hard work.	0	1	2	I model team qualities such as cooperation, respect and enthusiasm.
25	I would rather spend my time doing my own work rather than training and coaching others.	0	1	2	I like teaching and training others and enjoy seeing them learning from my experence.
26	I don't thing I come across as very confident and self-assured.	0	1	2	I know I come across as confident and self-assured.
27	I maintain great self-control and rarely if ever lose my temper.	0	1	2	I must admit I lose my temper too often and have blasted people who have done something stupid.
28	Even when I do my best, I feel guilty about the things I did not do perfectly.	0	1	2	I am a confident and capable person. I do my best and move on.
29	I sometimes have trouble making up my mind, but I will after having analyized of all the posibilities.	0	1	2	I make up my mind quickly. I will choose the best of the available alternative, and get on with it.
30	I imagine I appear reserved, cautious and thoughtful to others.	0	1	2	I imagine I look outgoing, strong and decisive to others.

iMind² Behavioral Styles Assessment

#	(0) I agree MORE with the Statement on the Left	(1) I agree with both EQUILY		(2) I agree MORE with the Statement on the Right
31	When making a point, I seldom raise my voice or use my hands for emphasis.	0 1 2		I occasionally raise my voice and/or use gestures to make my point at work.
32	Talking to people in positions of authority makes me feel nervous, self-conscious, or unsure of myself.	0 1 2		Talking to people in positions of authority does not make me feel nervous, or unsure of myself.
33	My boss would probably say I am less assertive than others in the office.	0 1 2		My boss would probably say I am more assertive than others in the office.
34	At lunch-time, if my co-worker suggests going out for Chinese and I want Italian, We will likely end up going out for Chinese.	0 1 2		At lunch-time, if my co-worker suggests going out for Chinese and I want Italian, We will probably end up going out for Italian.
35	My pace is slow, measured and steady at work.	0 1 2		My pace is rapid at work - I accomplish a great deal in a short period of time.
36	I find it very difficult to say "NO" to the people I work with.	0 1 2		I have no problem saying "NO" to the people I work with.
37	I am not too confident, but I am thoughtful.	0 1 2		I am not always thoughtful, but I am self-confident,
38	I often feel people take advantage of me at work.	0 1 2		I never allow people to take advantage of me at work.
39	I like to take my time and 'smell the roses,' perhaps strolling along chatting with an associate.	0 1 2		I walk more rapidly than others and often need to make myself slow down just to keep pace with others.
40	I feel threatened when dealing with someone who is very assertive or aggressive.	0 1 2		I do not feel threatened "If they want aggressive, I'll give them aggressive!"

iMind² Behavioral Styles Assessment

#	(0) I agree MORE with the Statement on the Left	(1) I agree with both EQUILY			(2) I agree MORE with the Statement on the Right
41	I generally speak less at business meetings than most others in attendance.	0	1	2	I generally speak more at business meetings than most others in attendance.
42	I am patient and seldom in a hurry and, while no one likes lining up or experiencing slow service, it really doesn't kill me to wait.	0	1	2	I am always in a hurry and I am very impatient waiting in line. I get really annoyed by the slowness of waiters or idiot slow drivers.
43	I do not establish a particularly high level of eye contact with people at work.	0	1	2	I establish a high level of eye contact with people at work.
44	When I have a disagreement with people at work, I often let it go rather than force a confrontation.	0	1	2	When I disagree with someone, I tell them so, even though they do not like it.
45	I often feel guilty or anxious when asking others to do things at work.	0	1	2	I ask others to do things at work without ever feeling guilty or anxious.
46	I do have a problem accepting a compliment.	0	1	2	I have no problem accepting a compliment.
47	If I feel that my ideas or opinions might upset others, I won't express them.	0	1	2	I express my ideas and opinions at work, even though they may upset others.
48	I often "turn the other cheek."	0	1	2	I seldom "turn the other cheek."
49	At work, my philosophy is "It's not whether you win or lose it's how you play the game."	0	1	2	At work, my philosophy is more "Winning isn't everything, it's the only thing."
50	My priority is to "Get along."	0	1	2	My priority is to "Get it done."

iMind² Behavioral Styles Assessment

#	(0) I agree MORE with the Statement on the Left	(1) I agree with both EQUILY		(2) I agree MORE with the Statement on the Right
51	I am a realist.	0 1 2		I am an idealist.
52	I cannot often tell when a friend is sad.	0 1 2		I can always tell when a friend is sad.
53	I am a really bad joke and storyteller.	0 1 2		I am a good joke and storyteller.
54	I would prefer to participate in individual sports.	0 1 2		I would prefer to participate in team sports.
55	I seldom embrace my parents and children and tell them that I love them.	0 1 2		I often embrace my parents and children and tell them I love them.
56	I am direct and business-like with shop clerks, waiters and other service personnel.	0 1 2		I am very friendly and kind with shop clerks, waiters and other service personnel.
57	I am not really a very spiritual person.	0 1 2		I am a very spiritual person.
58	I am a loner.	0 1 2		I am a people person.
59	I seldom show my true feelings to friends and relatives.	0 1 2		I often show my true feelings to friends and relatives.
60	In my personal life, I make decisions carefully and slowly.	0 1 2		In my personal life, I am very spontaneous and at times rash in my decision-making.

iMind^2 Behavioral Styles Assessment

#	(0) I agree MORE with the Statement on the Left	(1) I agree with both EQUILY			(2) I agree MORE with the Statement on the Right
61	I like small gatherings and prefer the quiet life.	0	1	2	I like the night life. I love to party.
62	I am task-oriented and cautious in the decisions I make in my personal life.	0	1	2	I am people-oriented and will take what I view as calculated risks when necessary.
63	To be honest I am not interested in getting to know people better. I don't care what makes them tick.	0	1	2	My success in relationships comes in part from my genuine interest in others and what makes them tick.
64	I am not that intuitive, I go with what my friends and family say, not what they don't say.	0	1	2	I am very much in touch with how others are feeling and can usually "read between the lines."
65	My friends and family would say I am thinking-oriented.	0	1	2	My friends and family would say I am feelings-oriented.
66	When I am under stress or upset, I tend to brush other people off.	0	1	2	Even through I am under stress or feel very upset, I still take time for other people.
67	I really don't try to explain my actions or my behavior to friends and family.	0	1	2	I feel it is important to explain my actions and behavior to my friends and family.
68	In my personal life, I make decisions based on observable facts as well as my own opinions.	0	1	2	In my personal life, I make decisions largely based on the opinions and advice of others.
69	I am not really in touch with my friends' or family's feelings.	0	1	2	I am very much in touch with my friends' and family's feelings.
70	I do not take criticism well and often become defensive when criticized by my partner.	0	1	2	I can accept criticism from my partner with an open mind without becoming defensive.

iMind² Behavioral Styles Assessment

#	(0) I agree MORE with the Statement on the Left	(1) I agree with both EQUILY		(2) I agree MORE with the Statement on the Right
71	I appear reserved to others.	0 1 2		I appear outgoing to others.
72	I am less outgoing and fun-loving than most of my acquaintances.	0 1 2		I am more fun-loving and outgoing than most of my acquaintances.
73	I am uncomfortable saying the words, "I love you" to men, women and children.	0 1 2		I am comfortable saying the words, "I love you" to men, women and children.
74	I am not that easy to get to know in new or unfamiliar social situations.	0 1 2		I am very easy to get to know in new or unfamiliar social situations.
75	My conversations are more focused on facts and current issues.	0 1 2		My conversations are more focused on personal life experiences.
76	I have trouble saying "NO" to my friends and family.	0 1 2		I have no problem saying "NO" to my friends and family.
77	I do not drive particularly fast nor am I all that impatient in traffic.	0 1 2		I probably do drive too fast and am very impatient in traffic.
78	I do not like to speak publicly.	0 1 2		I enjoy speaking in public.
79	If a stranger offends me or infringes on my rights, I seldom make a fuss.	0 1 2		If a stranger offends me or infringes on my rights, I will make an issue out of it.
80	I tend to be speechless when I am left alone with a person I find really attractive.	0 1 2		When alone with a very attractive stranger, I have no problem speaking with him or her.

iMind^2 Behavioral Styles Assessment

#	(0) I agree MORE with the Statement on the Left	(1) I agree with both EQUILY	(2) I agree MORE with the Statement on the Right
81	I am generally a slow-paced, calm individual.	0 1 2	I am a high-energy, fast-paced individual.
82	When I experience poor service in a restaurant, I seldom complain directly to the server or manager.	0 1 2	When I experience poor service in a restaurant, I let the server or manager know about it immediately.
83	In an elevator, I seldom make an effort to talk with strangers.	0 1 2	In an elevator, I make an effort to talk to my fellow travellers.
84	I seldom raise my voice at home.	0 1 2	I often raise my voice at home.
85	If someone cuts in line in front of me, I rarely say anything.	0 1 2	If someone cuts in front of me in line, I will always say something.
86	If my neighbor makes too much noise, I am very reluctant to say anything to him or her.	0 1 2	If my neighbor makes too much noise, I will certainly communicate my annoyance to him or her.
87	When my child, spouse or partner indicates they are in disagreement with me and wish to follow their own path, I will support them.	0 1 2	When my child, spouse or partner charts out a course that I disagree with, I will fight to the end to make them see the light.
88	When a friend borrows something from me and forgets to return it, I feel uncomfortable reminding him or her about it.	0 1 2	When a friend borrows something from me and forgets to return it, I don't feel uncomfortable asking for it back.
89	I often stop myself from saying what is really on my mind.	0 1 2	I usually say exactly what is on my mind.
90	I would never use intimidation or manipulation to ensure that I get my way.	0 1 2	To be honest, I will use intimidation or manipulation to ensure that I get my way.

iMind² Behavioral Styles Assessment

#	(0) I agree MORE with the Statement on the Left	(1) I agree with both EQUILY		(2) I agree MORE with the Statement on the Right
91	I make up my mind slowly.	0	1 2	I make up my mind quickly.
92	I avoid confrontation as much as possible.	0	1 2	I confront people I disagree with.
93	In my personal life, my priority is to "get along."	0	1 2	In my personal life, my priority is to "be respected and admired."
94	I am more passive than assertive.	0	1 2	I am more assertive than passive.
95	I avoid too much direct eye contact.	0	1 2	I usually look others straight in the eyes.
96	I don't thing I come across as very confident and self-assured to my friends and family.	0	1 2	I know I come across as confident and self-assured to my friends and family.
97	If I have a friend who consistently shows up late for appointments, I will usually just shrug it off.	0	1 2	If I have a friend who consistently shows up late for appointments, I will express my frustration.
98	I maintain great self-control and rarely if ever lose my temper with my significant other.	0	1 2	I must admit I lose my temper too often with my significant other when they do something stupid.
99	If an overly critical relative throws veiled insults at me, I will try to avoid, rather than confront, them.	0	1 2	If an overly critical relative throws veiled insults at me, I tell them they are being rude and ask why?
100	I have difficulty accepting compliments and sometimes downplay my appearance or ability.	0	1 2	I embrace compliments and certainly do not downplay my appearance or abilities.

Completing the Score Sheet

1. Turn to page 88 and total your circled responses for Questions 1 through 25 inclusive. Enter this sum in the box marked with an uppercase "A" on the score sheet on page 99. Then turn to page 90 and total your circled responses for Questions 26 through 50 inclusive. Enter this sum in the box marked with an uppercase "B" on the score sheet. Then turn to page 93 and total your circled responses for Questions 51 through 75 inclusive. Enter this sum in the box marked with a lowercase "C." Then total your circled responses for questions 76 through 100 and place that sum in the box marked "D."

2. Now double the numbers you have entered in the boxes marked "A" through "D" in column one and place the products in the column two boxes marked Ep through As.

3. Finally, on line five, total the numbers you have entered in boxes "A" and "C" in column one and enter the sum in box "E." This is your EXPRESSIVENESS score. On line 6, total the numbers you have entered in boxes "B" and "D" in column one and enter the sum in box "A." This is your ASSERTIVENESS score.

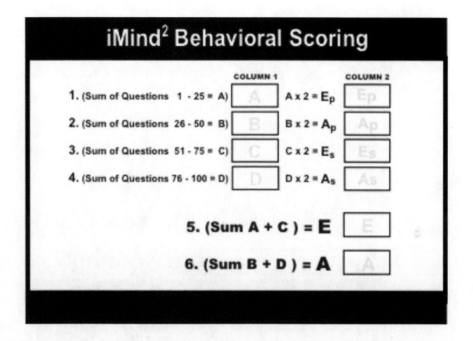

Mapping Your Score

To map your location on the Behavioral Styles Matrix found in
Appendix B, Page 236, follow these four steps:

Step One

Starting from the lower left-hand corner of the Behavioral Styles Matrix move up the vertical scale to the number you have written in the "E" (Expressiveness) box on the score sheet. Make a mark by that number on the vertical scale.

Behavioral Styles Matrix

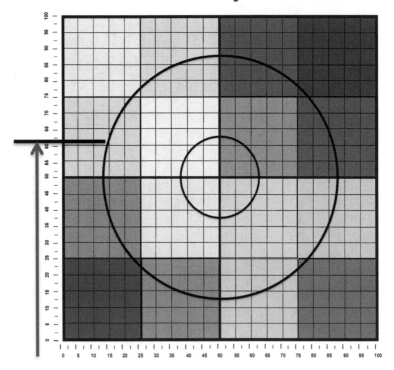

Step Two

Next, using a ruler or hard edge, draw a horizontal line across the
map through the mark you have made.

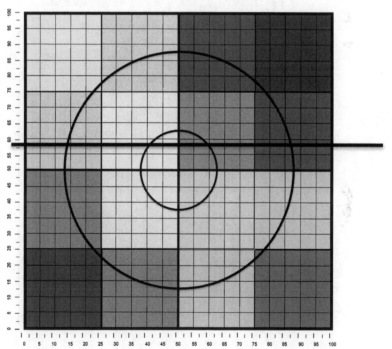

Behavioral Styles Matrix

Step Three

Then, starting from the lower left-hand corner (0) again, move across the horizontal scale until you reach your A (Assertiveness) score. Make a mark at this point on the scale.

Behavioral Styles Matrix

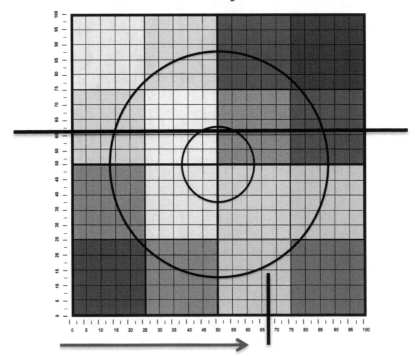

Step Four

Finally, using a ruler or straight edge, draw a vertical line all the way up the page through that mark.

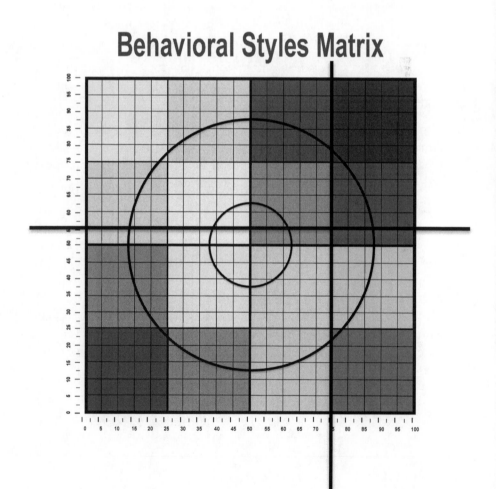

Behavioral Styles Matrix

It is the intersection of the two lines that you have drawn that indicates your location on the Behavioral Styles Matrix and which indicates your behavioral style.

Behavioral Flexibility

The iMind^2 has been carefully normalized. We have tracked tens of thousands of individuals who have taken the iMind^2, determining and applying the adjustments necessary to place precisely 25% of respondents within each of the four behavioral quadrants.

Also, your specific location within your behavioral styles quadrant is relevant. The closer you are to the center, the more you take on the characteristics of all four styles.

You will note that there are two concentric circles located on the Behavioral Styles Matrix. These concentric circles define and separate the three zones of behavioral flexibility and correlate more or less with one and two standard deviations.

Statistically, 10% of individuals completing the iMind^2 fall within the inner circle or what I call the "inner circle of flexibility." If you are one of these people, you might interpret this score to mean that you are more flexible than 90% of the population. People who fall within this inner circle tend to have less conflict in relationships; at least their behavior and the demonstration of their style tend not to precipitate conflict with others. It's much easier for these individuals to deal with people who fall within the other three styles because they have elements of each of those styles within their own personality.

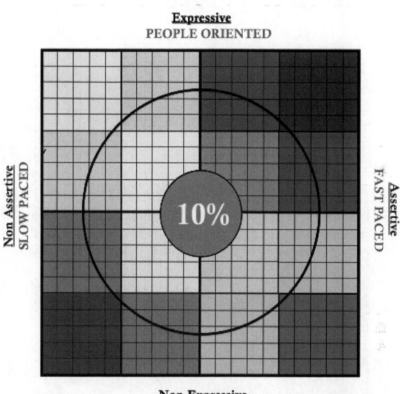

Of the people who take the test, 90% will score in that doughnut area that we might define as falling between the two concentric circles. Most people fall within this range. If you are one of those people, which is likely, the work that we're going to do with this model and having an understanding of this model can help you a great deal in understanding why it is that you have particular problems with certain types of people. It might also give you some insight into how you might improve your relationships with those people by temporarily taking on some of their characteristics.

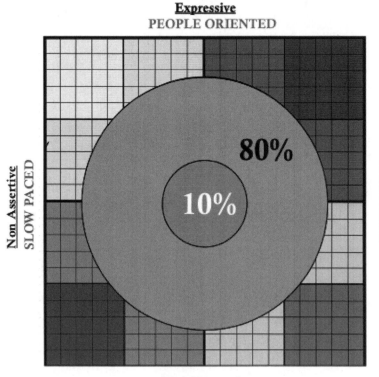

Behavioral Styles Matrix

Expressive
PEOPLE ORIENTED

80%

10%

Non Assertive
SLOW PACED

Assertive
FAST PACED

Non-Expressive
TASK ORIENTED

Of those taking this test, 10% will score outside the second concentric circle. This would indicate greater inflexibility than 90% of the population. If you scored in this zone, it does not mean that you're a bad person; it simply means that you're going to be constantly challenged throughout your life by those people who are diametrically opposed to you.

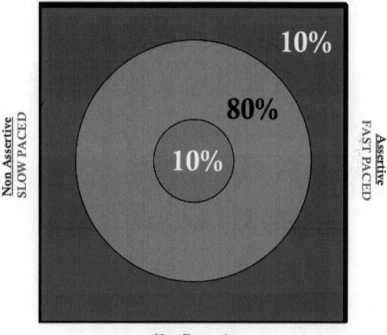

Behavioral Styles Matrix

The behavioral styles concept and the strategies for success with people, which you will learn in Chapter 9, can help you a great deal to negate this behavioral inflexibility.

It may appear that conflicts arise only with people whose styles differ from our own. This is not altogether true; major conflicts can also arise when we communicate, negotiate, or otherwise interact with people whose behavioral style is the same as our own.

Two thinkers working on a project will tend to feed each other's need for ever-increasing detail and data. Two dreamers may become easily distracted. Two supporters, wanting to avoid conflict and not rock the boat, may result in commitment to an agreement with which they are not really pleased. When two commanders come together, the strength of their personalities and their goal and task orientation can get in the way and lead to intransience, if not open combat. They can become like two rams bashing their heads together, neither willing to back down.

I've often seen this latter behavior in the relationship between an administrative professional and his or her boss, both of whom are commanders. The boss says, "I want you to do this," to which the administrative professional replies, "Not likely"; even if she doesn't say it, she is thinking it.

So we can see that there can be interpersonal conflicts with people who are different from us, and there can also be conflicts with people who are very similar to us.

What can be done?

Chapter 6

Time-Styles

In the preceding chapter, you determined your individual behavioral style, that is, your preferred way of interacting with the world around you. In this chapter, we will take the discussion further by identifying your specific time style.

Time style correlates highly with behavioral style but is seldom identical to it in that an individual's time style reflects learned vs. innate behaviors.

On the pages that follow, you will be presented with 25 statements followed in each case by four alternative options or choices. Please carefully read each statement and the choices provided and place an "X" in the box adjacent to the sub-statement that best reflects your belief or behavior.

Remember, you do not have to adhere fully to any of the options provided. It is just a matter of identifying which of the four sub-statements is the <u>MOST</u> acceptable to you.

When you are ready, please turn the page and complete the Time-Style Inventory.

Time-Style Inventory

Instructions:

For the 25 items below, please read each of the following four statements carefully, then place an X in the box adjacent to the statement that best reflects your belief or behavior.

1 In terms of the management of my time at work:

A	B	C	D

I am thorough. I take time to analyze and evaluate carefully.

I handle multiple tasks well and often think of new ways to do things.

I devote a lot of my time to helping others and move projects along by means of active listening.

I accomplish tasks quickly and have little difficulty staying on course.

2 When I am asked to take on a task or project when I am already over-committed, I will usually:

A	B	C	D

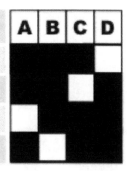

Say "no" unless I perceive this project to be both urgent and important.

Determine where this new project will fit in terms of my other current priorities.

Say OK if it looks interesting or will increase my visibility.

Take it on because it is hard to say no, but feel anxious about how this may affect my other commitments.

3 Which of the following organizational abilities best describes you at work?

A	B	C	D

I inspire and motivate others to move the project forward.

I accomplish tasks quickly and have no problem staying on course.

I move projects along by listening actively and adapting to others' ways of handling matters.

I pay attention to detail and follow procedures.

4 Which of the following best describes your workplace belief

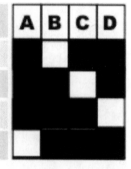

Because of my desire to help others accomplish their goals, I sometimes subordinate my own needs and desires.

Because of my perfectionism, I often take too long to accomplish a task, sometimes losing track of the goal.

Because of my strong desire to accomplish a great deal quickly, I occasionally ignore important details.

I tend to become easily bored and distracted when things bog me down, and tend to jump from one activity to another.

5 People procrastinate different things; I feel when it comes to the following, I tend to procratinate most often.

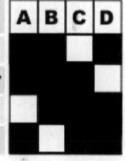

Decision making: because I feel it is important to have all the facts possible before making an important commitment.

Delegation: because I feel it takes as long to explain what I want, and show someone how to do it, as it would to just do it myself.

Planning and solitary action: such as working on a budgetary problem. I find this type of activity boring and tedious.

Confrontational situations: such as telling a boss or subordinate that I have a problem with his or her behavior.

6 My personal workspace:

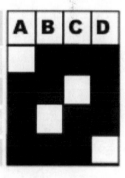

May look disorganized to others in the office, but I know where everything is, and I will neat things up one of these days.

Is functional, with a place for everything and everything in its place. I can't stand clutter.

I hope looks warm and inviting. I want visitors to relax and feel comfortable and welcome.

Matches my authority with enough space to spread things out and identify priorities without distraction.

7 After I have given an assignment to a subordinate:

I will occasionally ask him or her for an informal project report.

I will encourage him or her with a good deal of praise.

I will ask specific questions about his or her progress on the assignment and will often seek a project report.

I will often involve myself in the project to get him or her over the hump or help them deal with issues they may not be familiar with.

8 When I am in the middle of an important project and I hear a ding indicating I just got an email, I will usually:

Ignore it. It is more important to get the important project finished. It's just a matter of priorities.

Leave it for now. I check my emails at specific times during the day. I will also make a note to self to turn off my email alerts.

Check it out; it could be that someone needs something from me now, or it could be a message from a friend.

Open it up immediately; I am always curious and, come on, a two minute break won't make any difference to my day.

9 When I am assigned a major project at work, I usually begin by:

Running my ideas and intended approach by other people.

Determining and collecting all the data and information I will need.

Seeking input from my team.

Just jumping right in with both feet!

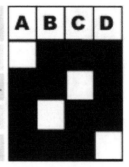

10 When someone drops in unexpectedly to, "just say hello," I usually:

Feel distracted because I have so many things in my head at the moment and don't want to lose my focus on the problem.

Find it hard to hide my impatience to get back to the project I was working on. I may be abrupt with them.

Take this opportunity to catch up on his or her life and see how he or she are doing. It is important to take time for others.

Kick back and enjoy the break, maybe have a laugh, it's only human.

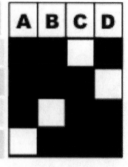

11 Which of the following adjectives best describes you at work?

Influencial.

Systematic.

Driven.

Amiable.

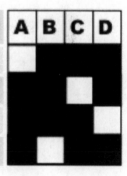

12 Which of the following best describes your belief or understanding of your own behavior at work?

I would rather work as a member of a team than work alone. My pace is rapid; I walk, talk and move quickly.

I would rather work individually on a project than work as a team member. My pace is rapid; I achieve a lot in a short time.

I would rather work as a member of a team than work alone. My pace is slow, measured, and steady.

I would rather work individually on a project than work as a member of a team. My pace is slow, measured, and thoughtful.

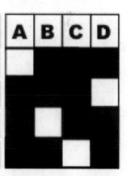

13 Which of the following best describes you?

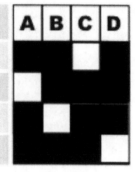

I view time in an orderly and objective way.

I frequently underestimate how long it will take to do something and often find myself rushing to complete tasks.

I may fall behind in my own work because I often take on other people's problems and priorities.

I have great concentration and prefer to work on one project at a time - without interruption.

14 If I were given the assignment of acquiring a major piece of equipment, I would most likely proceed by:

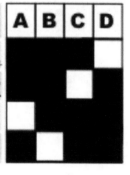

Determining the specifications required, creating a short list that meets the specifications, then quickly evaluating and buying.

Reading all the reviews available, checking the Web, researching, calling for tenders, then taking some time to really think about it.

Checking out the choices available, listening to what the salespeople have to say, then going with my gut feeling.

Talking to a number of my colleagues and associates, reading testimonials, maybe asking my boss's opinion; then praying.

15 Which one of the following time-management weaknesses best applies to you the most.

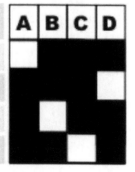

I become easily bored and distracted and accept too many interruptions.

My failure to delegate results in me being overwhelmed at times.

My inability to say "no" results in me being overwhelmed at times.

I am a perfectionist and know that I tend to procrastinate when it comes to decision-making.

16 One of my time-management problems is:

I am not very well organized and tend to procrastinate when it comes to planning.

Because of my desire to serve others, I sometimes leave too little time for my own priorities.

I recognize I often take too much time to make decisions.

Sometimes I don't ask for help when I should and may also occasionally fail to pay as much attention to detail as I should.

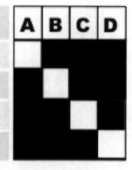

17 Faced with multiple tasks in my personal life:

I always begin with the task that best serves my priorities.

I begin with the one that is the most pressing.

I begin with the one that will benefit my friends or family the most.

I begin with the one that is the most interesting or fun.

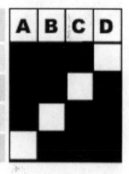

18 With regard to conversations and discussions, I like it best when:

They are lively, with a lot of ideas thrown out and allow me to openly express my opinions.

The group evaluates each alternative carefully, one by one.

Everyone, even shy and less assertive people, have an opportunity to participate and contribute.

People get to the point quickly.

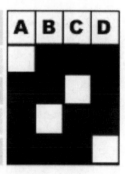

19 When I am working on an important project and a colleague offers his or her assistance:

Even though they are well intentioned, I am somewhat hesitant as he or she will not likely do it to my standards.

I would likely decline, it usually takes me as long to explain what I need, and he or she probably won't do it the way I would.

I am reluctant to a say yes, I don't want to be a burden on anyone, but he or she might also be offended if I say no.

I would happily agree; after all, "two heads are better than one," and it will be less work for me.

20 When I am chairing a meeting:

I find we often end late because of all the participation and give-and-take I have generated.

I feel satisfied when all the agenda items are covered well.

I will limit discussion and keep the group focused, so we can wrap up on time, having accomplished something.

I am happy when everyone participates.

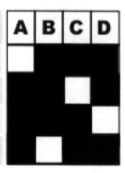

21 In terms of the way in which you manage your time, which is the greatest stressor for you?

Wanting things done now and having people insist we first go through a lot of unneccessary analysis or research.

Being distracted from your main focus by interruptions and other people's requests and priorities.

Being asked to do favors for others or being co-oped into a project that is not a priority for you and being unable to say "no."

Spending too much time in meetings or being forced to spend time on something that is illogical.

22 When I am working on an important project and the
phone rings, I would likely:

Let the machine get it. I can review it and return the call
later if necessary.

Answer it. It could be important and I can always use a break.

Answer it. It could be someone who really needs my help, and
besides, it is kind of rude to ignore a ringing phone.

Let it ring. I am working on something I know is important and
don't need to be interrupted by something that is probably not.

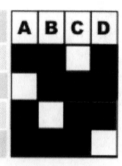

23 As I approach the paperwork in my in-basket, I usually
begin by:

Determining which item with the highest priority as well as
importance and then starting there.

Going through the pile, analyzing how long each item will take,
and then determining in terms of my schedule when to do what.

Starting with the item or request that looks to be the most
interesting or exciting.

Responding first to the requests of others.

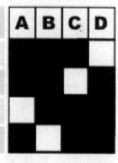

24 When a friend or loved one brings me a problem that he
or she is having, I am more likely to do the following:

Listen for a moment or two and then describe a similar
experience I had and how I successfully dealt with it.

Listen for a few minutes, then tell him or her what they need
to do.

Listen carefully for what he or she seems to be feeling so I can
lend support and hopefully so assistance in solving it.

Listen very carefully so I can make an intelligent suggestion or
recommendation to him or her.

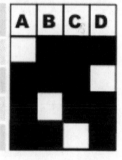

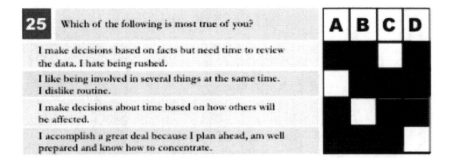

Having now completed the Time Style Inventory, please complete the score sheet below by simply adding the number of times you marked each column:

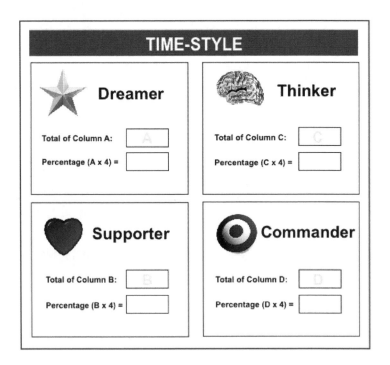

Your time style flows naturally from your individual behavioral style, which is the style indicated on your iMind^2 score sheet. However, your time style is not altogether the same as your behavioral style. Your time style reflections are, in large measure, learned behaviors. For this reason, you may find that your iMind^2 score and your time style score are not altogether in concert. In the workplace, we try new behaviors, methods, and approaches. Sometimes, these innovations work and, if they do, they are reinforced and adopted over time; other times they fail and, over time, they will be extinguished and abandoned.

While each of us has the ability to operate from each of the four time styles, one style tends to be dominant. This is reflected by the largest number and percentage on the score sheet on page 118.

Chapter 7

Time Challenges and the Four Styles

As you discovered at the end of the last chapter, you have a dominant style, which is one style that indicates, more than the others, a preference for the way in which you process information and interact with the world around you.

Some people think in terms of the big picture the grand design!—while others are more focused on specific goal accomplishment and the bottom line. Some people take a logical and systematic approach to problem solving, while others are only comfortable when decisions are reached through group consensus.

Individuals from each of the four time styles approach organization and time management differently. In fact, there are vast differences in terms of the way in which they organize themselves, set priorities, manage emails, create "to do" lists, etc.; but great differences also appear in terms of the ways in which they interact with others at meetings, when delegating responsibility, or in saying "NO," just to mention a few.

Having worked with nearly 100,000 executives, managers, and administrative professionals over the past four decades, I have not only been able to identify the top 12 time management problems faced by these individuals—what I call "Douglas' Dirty Dozen"—but I have also been able to correlate the issues and problems they have expressed with the four time styles. This information is provided below:

DOUGLAS' DIRTY DOZEN

1	Planning & Prioritization
2	Organization
3	Socializing Interruptions
4	The Telephone
5	Email & Internet
6	Procrastination
7	Handling Paperwork
8	Meetings
9	Delegation
10	Perfectonism
11	Unable to say "No"
12	Focus & Forgetfulness

Time-Style Problem Identification Chart

	Dreamer	Supporter	Thinker	Commander
Planning & Prioritization				
Organizing				
Socializing Interruptions				
The Telephone				
Email & Internet				
Handling Paperwork				
Meetings				
Delegation				
Perfectionism				
Unable to Say "No"				
Focus & Forgetfulness				
Procrastination				

Seldom a Problem Area for You

Occasionally a Problem Area for You

Often a Problem Area for You

(Please see color plate on page 237)

The Dreamer

Dreamers' fast-paced, extroverted personality and passionate, spirited style add value to most organizational situations. Their enthusiasm is contagious and often leads to a higher level of performance and commitment on the part of their fellow workers. They are usually the most creative of the four styles, adapt well to changing conditions and work environments, and can motivate and inspire others to perform at higher levels.

They enjoy entrepreneurial activities and, of course, networking with other people. For this reason, they often gravitate toward occupations that require creative or entrepreneurial thinking and that do not demand a great deal of theoretical knowledge or attention to detail.

Dreamers like center stage. They like to be noticed and involved. Dramatic and sometimes flamboyant, dreamers bristle with energy. They want to be continually on the go, and often find a desk too confining. They dislike long meetings.

Given a choice between doing things alone or with other people, dreamers will often choose the group activity. They tend to spend more time on the telephone than most people and also, of course, enjoy socialization activities.

They have a bold vision and they think big. They dream big dreams but implementation is left to other people.

Their impulsiveness often requires redos and/or apologies. They work according to opportunity rather than plan and are often late for meetings or miss them altogether. Because of distractions, they are often behind schedule on projects, miss deadlines, or come in just under the wire. Their interests are often eclectic. Expressive, good-natured, and playful, they can de-escalate conflict with humor.

Dreamers, however, have difficulty in a number of areas. When it comes to time management, they tend to leap before they look, acting in the absence of full and complete information. They become easily bored and distracted, often jumping from one activity to the next, particularly when a project or task bogs them down or appears, from their perspective, to be less challenging or interesting than other options.

Dreamers' approach to time management reflects their approach to life in general—flexible and unstructured. While this spontaneity can be of great organizational value, it can also create for them a trap inasmuch as in responding to the immediate, they can miss other goals and timelines.

The following are the areas that offer the greatest time management challenges for dreamers:

Planning and Prioritization

Dreamers often act prematurely or in the absence of complete information or data because of their preference for action, and their disdain for unsocial and arduous activities, such as planning.

Dreamers prefer action to planning. Solitary activities, such as planning and the analysis of alternatives, are replaced by action and involvement.

Dreamers tend to prioritize according to their interests in a particular project, rather than the relative importance of that project. For that reason, they tend to procrastinate when it comes to activities of a consequential nature.

Because dreamers are more concerned with the "what" than the "how," they are continually building castles in the air, and these, of course, are without foundation.

If you are a dreamer, try to choose your projects more carefully and recognize that things will usually take longer than you expect. Therefore set deadlines or better yet have others set them for you. Try to have fun at work and always have a project that you look forward to.

Organization

Dreamers are the most disorganized of the four behavioral styles. Their desks are typically the messiest and, while they will tell you that they know where everything can be found, to others, their desktops appear to be archeological digs.

The extent of their disorganization and its impact goes far beyond a messy desk. Deadlines are often missed because there are no adequate systems in place to remind dreamers of required actions or impending deadlines.

Dreamers typically fail to consistently employ organizations' systems or tools. If they make "to do" lists at all, they will likely do so on Post-it® Notes or scraps of paper.

Everyone has a natural preference for controlling time or adapting to it. People who try to control it need to be more adaptive and those who adapt to it need to control it more.

As a dreamer you should strive to keep a clear workspace, something you typically tend not to do. Force yourself to consistently use a date-book or electronic organizer where you can record a running "to do" list.

Don't be so relaxed when it comes to organization, self discipline is needed.

If you are fortunate enough to have an assistant to help you, choose that person carefully, to ensure they complement your unique time-style.

Interruptions

Dreamers are assertive and certainly have the ability to say no to interruptions, but they need to be engaged results in an accepting too many interruptions.

If a conversation is taking place within earshot, dreamers will have one ear on that conversation, creating a distraction from the project or task at hand. Likewise, a ringing telephone has a great sense of urgency for dreamers and must not be ignored. Typically, dreamers will check their emails throughout the day rather than at specific times.

Perhaps the greatest problem of all is that when a project begins to bog dreamers down or become boring or repetitive, they will often simply jump to a new or more stimulating task or project . This, of course, leaves tasks undone or requires them to be redone by others.

Telephone, Email, and Internet

As mentioned above, dreamers are enticed by a ringing telephone or the ding of an e-mail alert. They also spend more time than average surfing the Internet or engaging in social networking activities during work hours.

Scheduling

Dreamers schedule tasks and projects according to their interests rather than their importance. This can result in them wasting their "prime time," doing things of relative unimportance rather than attacking the most complex tasks during those hours of the day when their minds are most alert and their concentration is at its peak.

Focus and Forgetfulness

Dreamers' focus is often scattered. They have so many things on the go at one time that it is difficult for them to focus or concentrate with laser-like precision on any one activity. Information overload contributes to their forgetfulness. Because they personally have their hands in so many projects, while also tracing and monitoring the work of other team members, things get missed.

Dreamers need to stay with their #1 goal until it is completed.

This lack of focus and concentration takes a toll on dreamers. They seek and are animated by the praise of others, praise that they fail to receive when they fail to meet deadlines or continually change horses midstream. This can lead to anxiety and depression, which tends to afflict dreamers more than many of the other styles. Their highs are high but their lows are very low.

With regard to memory, they have difficulty remembering people's names. This stems, in part, from the fact that they are more interested in what they themselves have to say than in what others are saying. This failure to listen causes them to literally not hear the names of the individuals to whom they are introduced.

Dreamers are often good public speakers but their tendency to "wing it" or speak off the cuff rather than plan and rehearse their comments can result in them failing to cover everything that is required.

The Supporter

Supporters are thoughtful and cooperative team players. They do not seek the limelight; in fact, they are often content to bask in the glow of the accomplishments of others.

Supporters' willingness to compromise and their peacemaker approach to conflict can be valuable in high-pressure work environments.

Rather than leaping before they look, supporters give situations a sober second thought, ensuring that their actions will not in any way erode their relationships or harm others.

Supporters are good and loyal friends. They seek close personal relationships with other people, and they are patient, diplomatic, and dependable.

Good listeners, as their name suggests, they are highly supportive of others. This has great utility in modern organizations because it drives and encourages others toward completion.

We are all driven, in part, by the socialization processes that we have experienced in childhood. We are instilled with, and to some degree animated by, certain messages received as children. Be strong, be perfect, hurry up, stand out, and, in the case of supporters - please others.

The result of feeling that you must please others is that you will tend to put their priorities ahead of your own. Paradoxically, often the more time you spend serving the needs of others, the guiltier you will feel that you have not done enough. In other words, your need to please others can never be satisfied by trying to satisfy it.

Supporters seek harmony. They want to live personally harmonious lives but they also want others to feel as if they belong and, therefore, when it comes to task accomplishment, they seek to involve others in harmonious ways. Not surprisingly, most supporters' time management problems are found at the edge of their interactions with other people. The following represent the areas of greatest difficulty for supporters:

Planning and Prioritization

The supporter's problem is not so much with planning as with prioritization. Supporters, in fact, engage in significant planning activities. However, because they are such kind, concerned individuals, they tend to serve others' priorities before their own.

This can be particularly problematic where there is a significant power differential such as that of an administrative assistant and his or her boss.

If you are a supporter, try to give greater priority to your own goals, balancing the needs of others with your own.

Most importantly, try not to be all things to all people.

Telephone, Email, and Internet

Supporters spend more time on the telephone than is necessary, not wishing to employ termination techniques that may appear rude or dismissive to their callers.

They may also choose to speak on the telephone rather than send an e-mail or text message because they feel it's more personal.

Supporters will answer a ringing phone regardless of the importance of the task at hand as they do not wish to appear rude and also because they worry that the caller may need something that only they can provide.

Supporters' e-mails tend to be longer than necessary and often invite unnecessary responses or follow-up.

Social networking can be a problem for supporters but is typically not as great a problem as it is for dreamers.

Interruptions

In addition to the problems caused by telephone and e-mail interruptions, drop-in visitors are an issue for supporters. Their door is always open.

When a drop-in visitor approaches them with "Have you got a minute?" they invariably say yes. Additionally, once the drop-in interruption begins, supporters have difficulty terminating the visit. They feel that comments such as, "George, you will have to excuse me. I need to get back to work now," or "Sally, is there anything else I can do for you before we end?" are too direct or rude.

Procrastination

Everyone procrastinates around their non-preferences which for the Supporter is confrontation.

Inability to Say "NO"

Perhaps the greatest challenge that supporters face is their inability to say no. This results in them often being overwhelmed. Supporters want everyone to feel good about themselves, to experience high levels of self-esteem, and to have their needs satisfied. The problem, however, is that they will often subordinate their own needs to the needs of others.

By placing the needs of others ahead of their own, resentment often builds in their lives and, in the end, the feelings of being used can be destructive to their relationships.

The Thinker

Thinkers are logical and systematic. When they do a job, they do it right by employing the scientific method. They determine and establish all the alternatives, they evaluate each of those alternatives, and then they choose the most critical path to the attainment of the optimal alternative or solution. There are few organizations today, either private or public, whose detailed and organized approach is not valued and needed. Thinkers' determination to get it right makes them essential to organizational success.

Thinkers are problem solvers. They are tenacious in seeking out the best solution. You might give them a problem and forget that you have given them a problem, but they don't forget, get bored, or jump to a less challenging task; instead, they hang on until a solution is found.

Thinkers' internal drivers say, "be perfect." This, too, may be a result of childhood programming and socialization. The fear of failure can make one thorough, but it can also lead to perfectionism, the need to do everything flawlessly, which is a high standard and one that is unachievable for any human being. The belief that you must be perfect in everything you undertake and the inevitable realization that you are not a perfect being can be damaging to your self-esteem. Also, the tendency to apply this standard to others, including your mate, can be highly destructive.

Traditional time management advice reaches an eager ear in the case of thinkers. As with most left-brain individuals, the use of "to do" lists, datebook organizers, and calendars comes naturally to thinkers.

If you are a thinker, organize your work into broad categories. Try setting deadlines sooner than they need to be.

The following areas present the greatest challenge to thinkers:

Interruptions

Like supporters, thinkers' non-assertive behaviors affect the way in which they deal with drop-in visitors. However, unlike supporters, they find it more difficult to hide their annoyance.

Thinkers operate with a sense of urgency and, for that reason, can ignore a ringing telephone or email alert when working on a project that requires their undivided attention.

Handling Paperwork

The problem that thinkers have with paperwork is that they simply generate too much. They certainly believe in CYA and certainly see greater efficacy in the written than the spoken word. They feel it is important to memorialize their activities with written notes and reports.

Meetings

Thinkers do not always see the value of meetings. They may not be fully engaged in the meeting as their mind is often filled with the projects waiting for them back in their own office.

Thinkers are particularly put off by individuals who ramble on in meetings or take such meetings as an opportunity to discuss matters of a personal nature, thereby taking the agenda off course. This is what the Cockneys call Jackanory, which is rhyming slang for "telling a story."

Meetings, at least good meetings, are meant to be platforms on which individuals who have apprised themselves of the facts can now make a decision. This approach in itself is problematic to thinkers, first because they rarely feel they have enough data on which to act and second, because they feel that additional thought is needed before a final decision is made

Perfectionism

Thinkers have only one way of doing a job, and that's perfectly. At times, this is altogether appropriate and even necessary. There are times, however, when a lower standard can be applied. The issue here is that the thinker has difficulty recognizing that not every task or project needs this exacting level of performance. At times, it appears that there is never a final version of a report or that closure can be given to a particular problem or issue.

If you are a thinker, occasionally stop halfway through a project to ask yourself if you are overdoing it.

Delegation

Thinkers' failure to delegate arises from their perfectionism. They feel, and often rightfully so, that no one else can meet their high standards or perform the task as thoroughly or completely as they would. They also believe that it would take as long to explain in detail what is required as it would to simply complete the task themselves. Since thinkers often underestimate the time involved in some activities, they can be impatient with those to whom they delegate.

The Commander

Commanders are strong, independent, and firm in action and decisions. When they set a goal, it is difficult to dissuade them from the accomplishment of that goal.

Commanders are also great persons to have in a crisis. They can make difficult decisions in a measured, rational, non-emotional way. They also make decisions quickly based on their innate cost-benefit approach to problem solving.

Their intent is to get the job done.

They are both pragmatic and efficient, providing them with a powerful administrative ability.

If there were one message that Commanders likely received as children, it was to "hurry up." The result of this programming is that they try to pack more and more into less and less time.

It is not surprising that statistically, the majority of "Type A" individuals come from this time style. Commanders certainly do not take time to smell the roses. They accomplish a great deal but not without it taking a toll in terms of stress and the quality of their relationships.

Commanders are keenly aware of time as well as its management, and, whenever possible, they prefer to have plans in place before the work has begun.

Traditional time management recommendations and techniques are well received by commanders. Their time management philosophy is in concert with the admonition found in Ecclesiastes—finishing is better than beginning.

If you are a commander, make sure you know what your mission is – your life's purpose. You are a good short-term planner but you also need to look at the big picture. Try to be more patient with yourself, don't beat yourself up if you occasionally miss a deadline. You have a problem delegating but try to think of it as a way to teach excellence to others.

The following areas can be challenging to commanders:

Meetings

Commanders are great people to have around in crises, but there direct style and approach can, at times, ignore advice given by others. They tend to bulldoze others and take an autocratic approach to the task at hand.

Delegation

Commanders have difficulty with delegation. They feel that it would take as long to explain their needs with regard to a project or task as it would to complete it themselves. They also tend to fear their subordinates' incompetence.

There is another fear that commanders have, and that is they fear their subordinates' competence. Commanders seek control, and by delegating responsibility to another, they are also increasing that person's power and decreasing their own.

Perfectionism

Commanders set very high standards for themselves. In effect, they keep raising the bar so that excellence becomes average and average becomes failure. They are continually seeking more and better and are very hard on themselves when they fail to reach the very high standards that they set for themselves.

This constant striving for perfection in all things can be highly destructive when applied to their relationships, both at work and at home.

Chapter 8

Cleaning Up the Dirty Dozen

1. Planning and Prioritization

In Chapter 1, we defined time management as the *act of controlling events*.

If greater control is our goal, if we seek to increase control in every aspect of life, including time management, we have to start with planning. It is planning or forethought that, in the long run, will result in the kind of control that can make a difference in our lives.

The great Peter Drucker said, "Action without planning is the reason for every failure."

For that reason, I would encourage you, if you have never done it, to sit down with a pen and a sheet of paper and try to determine what it is you're trying to accomplish, not just this week or next month, and not just in your career or financially, but in every aspect of your long-term life. Set lifetime goals if you haven't already done so.

These aren't New Year's resolutions. These are long-term goals that, if realized, will result in the kind of happiness and success for which you have always longed. Ask yourself this simple question: "What is it that I hope to accomplish in my life [and this is vitally important] based on my governing values?"

Not just "What kind of career do I want to be in?", not just "How much money do I want to have in the bank?", but also "What kind of relationship do I want to be in?", "Where do I want to be in terms of my recreational goals, my spiritual goals, my family goals?" Try brainstorming the questions. A brainstorm is where you ask a question and then record everything that comes to mind, no matter how ridiculous or even how impossible it seems. In fact, the strength of the brainstorming approach is that you have to postpone any negative thoughts or critical evaluations until later. What you're hoping for is that, free of all constraints, your mind will storm the questions. Write everything down. Don't stop yourself by thinking, "Oh, I couldn't do that," or "I'm not smart enough," or "I couldn't afford it," or "I'd have to go back to school," or "What would my husband or wife say?" If an idea enters your mind, write it down.

Although you may find that, at first, you are blankly staring at a sheet of paper, soon one idea will lead to another and you will fill the sheet and likely many more.

Don't be shy! What are your secret ambitions? What are the things that you have regretted not doing? Do you have secret wishes? How do you visualize your ideal life?

Now is the time to critically examine what you have written.

You will eliminate three types of goal statements:

1. Anything that is technologically impossible. I don't mean those things that are difficult; rather, I am referring to those things that are basically impossible. You may have written down, for example, that you want to be the first woman on the moon. That's probably impossible. You're probably starting too late for that kind of a career move or living in the wrong country. However, at this point, don't eliminate things that are difficult and call them impossible. These are precisely the type of things that you must plan to accomplish.

2. Next, recognize that it is very difficult and often highly stressful to do two things that are mutually exclusive; in fact, it is difficult to maintain a healthy state of mind while continually seeking to accomplish two things that draw you in diametrically opposed directions. It will only lead to great unhappiness in your life. Try to identify them and deal with the goal conflicts now.

3. Finally, eliminate the trivia. You may have written down something like "I want to own a certain type of automobile." Draw a line through those types of statements. They are too trivial. If this is important at all, it will come as a part of something greater, such as a financial goal.

Next, identify your major goal areas. You may have many or you may have only a few, but you will have some. Pluck out all the financial goals and put them together, identify relationship goals and put them together. Do the same for career, spiritual, recreational, etc. goals.

Now, and this is what takes some talent, compress all of the statements identified under each goal area into one clear and succinct paragraph each. Be sure the paragraphs are written in behavioral terms, i.e., something against which you can measure your progress, a statement that focuses on the behavior. Rather than ending up with a statement such as, "I want to be rich," you want a statement that is measurable and identifiable such as, "I want to be in a job earning $200,000/year within a decade," or "I want such and such in my bank account by my 40th birthday."

Is this type of very specific lifetime goal setting essential to the daily management of your time? Perhaps not, but there will be times in each of our lives when we might misstep if we don't know what is important to us based on our governing values.

When I worked through this process many years ago, I ended up with seven lifetime goals. You may have 10, you may have four; we are all different, but you will have at least a few.

Write these goals down somewhere where you can view them often. Put them in your iPhone™ or your datebook organizer. The rest is planning and scheduling.

Now that you have set your lifetime goals, each New Year's Day, rather than setting resolutions that you will likely forget in a week or two, look at your first lifetime goal and ask yourself: "What can I do in 201x to move me closer to the attainment of my first lifetime goal?" Write this sub-goal down: "I can't do it all this year. Hopefully, I will have more time—at least that is the plan—but I have to do something this year." Then look at your second lifetime goal and do the same thing, and so on. So if you have seven lifetime goals, you'll have seven sub-goals for this year.

Finally, at the beginning of each month, ask yourself the question, "What can I do in the month of March/February/December to move me significantly closer to the accomplishment of my first yearly sub-goal for this year?" Then tell yourself "I recognize I can't do it all this month, nor can I put all my eggs in this one basket, but I have to do something, no matter how small, this month." Then looking at your other yearly sub-goals, do the same.

Prioritizing

You can do anything you want; you just can't do everything you want. There just isn't enough time. You have to choose. You have to set priorities. To live a full and satisfying life, you have to decide what's important to you and arrange your time and activities accordingly.

The problem is, we all view priorities differently. To the dreamer, for example, everything can appear to be a priority, while the supporter often has difficulty separating other people's priorities from his or her own. Commanders, often having been brought up with the "hurry up" driver, naturally establish priorities according to the relative importance of the tasks and projects before them, while thinkers will expend a great deal of time just trying to determine what their priorities are.

If there's one prioritization tool, however, that all the styles need to adopt it's the "to do" list. It doesn't have to be elaborate, it doesn't have to be complicated; in fact, if we do complicate things too much, the action-oriented individual, the dreamer for example, will not do it for long.

I've seen many elaborate types of "to do" lists, but the simple ABC system is as good as any.

The essential elements of the ABC system are:

1. Make a list of everything that needs to be done today.

2. Prioritize the list according to A, B, and C.

     A - The things that must be done
     B - The things that could be done
     C - The things that shouldn't be done

3. Start with the "A"s and end with the "B"s.

4. Say no to the "C"s or fit them into travel, waiting time, etc.

Well, there is a little more to it than that.

When should this "to do" list be done? Many time management coaches will tell you that the answer to this is first thing in the morning. They counsel that when you enter the office in the morning, you should close the door, ignore phone calls and email messages, and shun co-workers. Rather, they suggest that you spend the first 15 minutes planning your day.

I think first thing in the morning is probably the worst time of the day to tackle the items on your "to do" list. The phone is typically ringing off the hook, email alerts are dinging, bosses and others are vying for your attention, and, of course, there is all that socializing that has to be done.

No. Unquestionably, the best time of day to plan your day is last thing in the day…for the next day, of course!

Why? Because at the end of the day, you can see clearly all those

things that you were unable to do today, often through no fault of
your own. People didn't get back to you with the information they
promised, things took longer than you anticipated, or a crisis threw
you off.

Also, if you forget to add something to your list, it will often come
to you before the next morning. I have found that in my experience,
by creating my "to do" list last thing in the day, my subconscious
will work overtime to provide greater insight into how to best tackle
a particular task or activity. I can't tell you how often I have woken
up with an idea or solution that applies to my work for that day.

Additionally, planning is not a task that requires a huge amount of
energy. For many of us, our most productive time is early in the
morning. Would it not be better to step into the accomplishment of
an important task during your best hours of the day rather than
squander any of it on an activity that can be done just as well during
a less productive period?

The question is often asked; "What makes an 'A' an 'A'?"

An "A" is a project or activity that:

1. Is important to your boss or leader
2. Offers visibility to you and your ideas and/or skills
3. If not done expeditiously, will create a bottleneck and other
   members of your team will be unable to achieve their goals
4. Is vital to the needs of your clients or customers

It is useful to view each of the items on your "to do" list in terms of
the activities matrix that we discussed earlier in the book. Where
does each item on your list fall? Is important and urgent is important
but not urgent is it not important but urgent or is it neither
important nor urgent.

"A"s are usually important and often urgent; "B"s may be important but are usually less urgent; and "C"s are usually not important but often urgent. Both commanders and thinkers have little difficulty with this approach.

But there will be some pushback from dreamers who prefer immediate gratification. Their natural tendency is to set priorities according to their likes and dislikes rather than the degree of importance of the task or activity. Considerable self-discipline is required here if the flexible freethinking dreamer hopes to accomplish more.

Supporters, on the other hand, are too willing to disrupt their plans to better accommodate the needs of others.

Planning and prioritizing helps us to get control of our time and our lives. To be successful, you need to have a clear vision of your life in the future. Instead of responding to life by giving in to the demands of others, continually reacting to crises, or simply doing things out of habit, we give up control.

Planning brings the future into the present and ensures that our goals become more than just pipe dreams. Defining your goals and objectives will help you to achieve your dreams or, at the very least, go a long way toward it. No, there isn't enough time to do everything, but there is always enough time to do what is important.

2. Organization

For some people, organization comes naturally. Their desktops are clear, their desk drawers contain only the tools and materials that they absolutely need, and their filing system is such that if they need to find something it can be in their hands within a minute.

For other people, disorder is the order of the day. They seem to thrive on clutter; their desktops have the appearance of an archaeological dig, and while they usually and eventually find what they need, a great deal of time is wasted searching. These individuals are often viewed as unprofessional by others.

For much of this discussion, I am speaking to dreamers, but we all suffer, to some degree, from this self-imposed time waster of disorganization.

Most people say that they want to be better organized because they realize that by so doing, they will have more time—time that they can spend productively doing things that matter. They also realize that better organization will provide them with a more professional image.

But just getting organized is not enough. Clearing your desktop or moving the rubbish in your desk drawers to the wastepaper basket is not enough. You need to focus on keeping things current, setting up procedures and standards that will maintain order in your environment. The point is to get organized and stay organized so that you can find what you want and what you need quickly and easily.

Without a doubt, dreamers have more of a problem with disorganization that the other three styles. This is not to say that the other three are by any means perfect in this regard; it is simply that, in most cases, the others may go through periods of disorganization, but their disorganization is not systemic as it is in the case of the dreamer.

When it comes to organization, there are three guiding principles:

1. Organize to support your goals and objectives
2. Create parking spaces— i.e., a place for everything—so that things
   can be kept in their place
3. Organize around your behavioral style

When you follow through on these three principles, particularly organizing to better achieve your objectives, you will achieve and maintain greater order in your life.

When I went to high school eons ago, boys were required to take a course call "Shop." It didn't matter that you had no interest in becoming a carpenter or woodworker, you had to take Shop. In Shop, we were required to make wooden birdhouses, coffee tables, or, in my case, a "knickknack" shelf.

My Shop teacher, like most of the Shop teachers I observed, seemed to be at the edge of emotional collapse. This was perhaps understandable since he had to manage a group of 40 disinterested adolescent boys in a room full of power tools.

I also remember spending what seemed like half of class time putting away our tools. This meant rehanging each of them on a specific hook provided for that particular tool. How could these "keeners" find that right spot? Because each tool had a painted outline of the tool stenciled below the hook. If it was a wrench, it had an outline of a wrench; if it was a chisel, it had an outline of a chisel.

When I'm talking about creating a place for everything and keeping things in that place, I'm not talking about this type of rigid structure. The whole point of the time style philosophy is that we choose systems and techniques that suit our style. Yes, there may be a period of adjustment and there may be some discomfort initially. But if we demand adherence to rules or systems that run contrary to an individual's natural preferences, in most cases they won't be implemented and, if they are, they will usually be discarded in short order. There is no single solution for everyone and very often you have to try different ways of organizing before you find one that suits your particular style. But in order to be organized, you have to get organized.

Think about your workspace right now. What does your desktop look like? Are your desk drawers stuffed full of everything you don't have a place for? Is your filing system adequate? Or do you have heavy stacks of paper on your desk and credenza on the floor?

Clutter can be emotionally draining, it can be stressful, and it is certainly a time waster. Hundreds of hours can and are consumed each year searching through files for misplaced information.

Many of us have come to realize that the paperless office is a myth—it always has been. Even with all the electronic devices we have today—computers, scanners, cell phones, etc.—there really hasn't been a significant reduction in the amount of paper with which most people in management have to deal. We may create our correspondence on computers but we still print them out and create copies for reference. We talk to people on our cell phones but often send written confirmations. We ask salespeople and suppliers to send us written quotes and even file copies of our emails as proof of action, and, to the delight of the photocopy companies, we send unnecessary copies of everything marked "for your information" to everyone!

The more paper that you keep, the more difficult it is going to be for you to work effectively. Time is wasted shuffling through all your papers looking for the piece that you need. It's been reported that the average office worker spends more than 45 minutes a day looking for papers before he or she can actually deal with them.

If you want to tame the "paper tiger," why not start with the "file or toss" session? If you don't have the time to spend an entire morning doing this, then why not set aside half an hour a couple times a week to attack this problem?

Incidentally, I would recommend that you do your decluttering on your own time and out of the view of your boss and colleagues. It is almost a tacit admission that you are, or have been, out of control. Most bosses don't like it. It's as if they are paying you twice—the first time to create the mess, and the second time to free yourself from it. You might also gather a crowd of your co-workers milling around asking questions like, "Are you getting rid of this?"

For your "file or toss" session, follow the five steps below:

You will need to assemble your "file or toss" tools:

1. A large wastepaper bin (most important).
2. Five cardboard boxes

3. File folders
4. Labels
5. Felt markers

Use your felt marker to label your boxes "action," "pending," "filing," "pass on," or "reading."

Begin by putting all stray papers—in fact, everything that doesn't have a place or isn't in its place—in a pile on the floor, tabletop, or other large piece of office furniture.

As you move items from their present resting place to this pile, you can now do your first screening. Throw away empty containers of anything, old calendars, misprinted business cards, convention handouts, rough drafts, homey touches, and sentimental crap.

Now go through each piece of paper one by one. The trick to clearing paper is that you deal with it one piece at a time.
As you do, ask yourself the following five questions:

1. "Is this item actionable now?" If the answer is yes and it simply requires a phone call, email, or short note, take that action. If more information is needed before you can make a decision, or more work is required to accomplish the task, drop it in the "pending" file.

2. "Will I ever need this piece of paper again?" If the answer is no, then drop it in the wastepaper basket. If you will need it, where should you file it? If the answer is yes and you have an existing file for materials of this type, put the item in the file now. If not, put it in a file folder and handwrite a description of the item. Drop it into the "filing" box. You or your assistant can type a proper label on the file folder later.

3. "Does this belong to someone else or is it of primary interest to someone else? Would he or she really want it?" If so, use your felt marker to write that person's name on it and drop it in the "pass on" box.

4. "Is this item something you want or need to read?" If yes, drop it in the "reading" box. But be sure that the information still relevant. We often put things aside because of a real short-term interest or motivation that we had but may not now have. Our interests are always in flux; if you no longer feel any sense of urgency to expand your knowledge of this area, then toss the item.

These four questions reinforce the fact that there are really only four things you can do with paperwork—deal with it, pass it on, file it, or toss it.

Dreamers, supporters, and commanders can do this. Thinkers almost always answer "no" to the first question and "yes" to the other three. They are reticent to take action in the absence of complete information and, for them, there is always more information to come. Likewise, their answer to the second question, "Will I ever need this paper again?" is "yes," "maybe," or "I don't know." Maybe a better question for the thinker to ask would be, "If this piece of paper fell out of my hands and into the wastepaper basket, what is the worst thing that could happen?" If you know where you can get another copy quickly, let it go. If it's no longer relevant or current, let it go. If someone else has the information filed away, let it go. If the chances are slim that you'll ever need to see it again, let it go.

There are really only four reasons to keep something:

1. It would be extremely difficult to get another copy

2. There are legal or regulatory reasons why retention is necessary

3. You originated the document

4. It is required for an ongoing project.

Also, try to stop paper before it gets to you. Get your name taken off as many junk mail lists as possible or write to the Mailing Preference Service, an organization that is equivalent to the telemarketing-related "do not call list" with which you are probably familiar. Try to take your name off internal mail lists that are not absolutely vital. Also, don't ask people to send you documents or copies that you really don't need just for the sake of confirmation. The same, of course, applies to e-mails but we will talk about those later.

Now, having pared down your paperwork and having at least organized the remainder into four categories, let's now find a place to park it.

I would recommend putting all the action items into a red file folder and placing it in a file folder holder on your desk. This will be the only folder on your desk, your primary work area.

Next, place all the items in the file marked "pending" and place this file in a close and convenient location, but not on your desk.

Then, take the files from your "filing" box and file them NOW.

If you are fortunate enough to have a secretary or administrative professional, ask that person to distribute the material in your "pass on" file to the appropriate individual at his or her convenience.

The "to read" material should be placed as far away as possible from your desk and at least out of your line of sight so as not to become a distraction. You might want to put it in your briefcase so that you can read it while you are on a flight or waiting for a meeting to start, etc.

Workspaces

You have essentially two work spaces to organize. The first is your desk. This is your primary work area. The second is bookcases, cabinets, tabletops, credenzas, etc.

Your primary workspace needs to be organized so that everything you need is within reach—the telephone, staplers, paperclips, pens, markers, pads etc. but nothing else. This is prime real estate; you don't want low-priority items in high-priority space.

Also, as we have already mentioned, you want to have just the "action" file on your desktop and, before you, the material related to the action item on which you are currently working.

For most of us, more and more of our time is spent in front of a computer screen. It is important, therefore, that your computer is conveniently located, requiring, at the very most, a swivel to reach it.

Maintain an in-basket into which you or your assistant can place incoming mail and other items for you, and an out-basket for the documents that you have completed.

Organizational Tools and Techniques

Perhaps the single most important tool in your time management toolkit is a time planner. A planner, whether it's a paper datebook organizer or its electronic equivalent, is essential. This tool enables you to plan for the year, the month, the week, and, of course, each day ahead. It allows you to keep all of your contacts in one place. It has a calendar enabling you to schedule activities and appointments months in advance, and, of course, it has a place for you to create your "to do" list.

I think it's important to always work from a list, and that list has to be in front of you. The problem that many of us have is that we accept assignments, we delegate work to others, people call us with information, and we scribble all this information down on random scraps of paper or Post-it® notes. This information then swirls around our offices, in and out of our briefcases and our in-baskets, and a lot of it simply gets lost between the cracks.

The first organizational principle, when we speak to the use of a planner, is that we put everything in one place. Your planner needs to be comprehensive enough to have a place for everything we mentioned above.

The second principle is that your planner needs to be portable. You want to take it everywhere with you. You want it by the side of your bed at night so that if a brilliant thought comes to you in the middle of the night, you can record it. You want it in your pocket or purse so that if it at lunch you have to set an appointment, you can check your availability and you can plug that person in.

It's important to have a place in your organizer for your "to do" list. I use an electronic organizer. Today, there are, of course, so many apps out there for reminders and "to do" lists. They make it easy to enter tasks and tick them off once they have been accomplished. Notice I said "tick them off", not "delete them." One of the advantages of recording your "to do" list in your organizer is that it gives you, in at least précis form, a diary, a record of your accomplishments. You can generally go back and reconstruct much of what you did and when.

Tickler System

A simple "bring forward" or "tickler system" can help to decrease the chances of that in-basket pile getting higher and higher again. Most of us have desk drawers that double as a small file cabinet. I would suggest getting 45 file folders and file hangers to put in that space. Label 31 folders 1 through 31 for each day of the month and label another 12 file folders with each of the months of the year. The last two file folders are labeled next year and the year after that.

Now when a request or piece of correspondence arrives at your desk that needs action on particular date, you can simply open the drawer and drop it in the appropriate file folder. If it is relevant to a particular day this month, drop it in that file folder. If it's for another month, put it in the relevant file folder. At the beginning of each month (or year), of course, you take everything out of that file folder and place the contents either into your "action" file or into the appropriate file for the day (or month). This system takes a very short time to set up and helps to ensure that you deal with matters in a timely manner and that you don't miss appointments, insurance policy renewals, etc.

3. Socializing Interruptions

Another time waster for which dreamers lead the pack, both as sufferer and instigator, is socializing interruptions. Supporters also have a problem in this area but are rarely the initiators.

We all know the question, "You got a minute?" These are probably the five deadliest words spoken in today's office environment. It's rarely a minute—in fact, it's rarely 10 minutes. It really translates to, "Can I interrupt you for an indeterminate period of time?"

To eliminate this time waster, you have to recognize that these minutes that are being requested add up to months and years of wasted time.

Socializing is a normal part of the work experience, especially if you are successful and talented. It's only natural for your staff and colleagues to want to talk to you if you can help them with their work.

Whether it's to answer questions, provide guidance, or set people in the right direction, lending support to others can be a valuable service to your team and your organization.

However, people often descend on you solely to satisfy their need to interact with another human being for reasons unrelated to their work or your expertise.

Socializing interruptions can be a tremendous drain on your time and can interfere with your concentrated focus on your work.

The key to handling this type of interruption effectively is to distinguish whether the interruption and your response to it have utility for the organization or are simply serving someone's need for company.

It is important to take steps to reduce the latter, both in terms of their number as well as their frequency.

If you take the time to run a time log, as we recommended earlier, you will discover that 80% of your socializing interruptions are caused by about 20% of your co-workers and colleagues. These are your habitual socializers. They don't seek your help or guidance, nor do they really want to get to know you better; they are simply looking for an excuse to procrastinate or kill some time. They want to socialize when you want to work.

And please, I am not suggesting that you seek to eliminate all socializing. In any workplace, people need to socialize. It improves morale and camaraderie and is an important part of effective team building. However, you may need to increase your control in this area. Like everything else, balance is the key.

If you want to improve in this area, you will need a strategy to deal effectively with drop-in visitors. The following strategies can help:

1. Try to be less inviting. Instead of welcoming them with a friendly question, you may need to discourage the interruption. For example:

Drop-in: "Hi, got a minute?"

You: "I'm swamped right now. Is it something urgent?" or

You: "Jack, I am actually. I'm in the middle of something right now. Can it wait?"

Most of your habitual socializers will conclude that you don't have any interest in socializing and find someone else to talk to.

2. Stand up when speaking to the visitor. Sitting down results in drop-ins feeling more relaxed and not so rushed, and also makes it more difficult for you to get them out of that chair once they have sat down. Most people will not sit while you're standing because we all feel more comfortable when at the same eye level. Also, by standing, you can dance them toward the door when the time is right.

3. Move the interruption out of your space: "Janet, I am absolutely swamped right now, I'll drop by your office when I get a chance." By moving the interruption out of your space and into hers, you can better control it; first, by moving the interruption to a time that suits you, and, second, it is much easier for you to retreat than remove the drop-in from your office. Likewise, a response, such as, "Let's talk just before the planning and review meeting starts this afternoon," or "Let's talk at the coffee break," is effective.

3. Close your door or at least shift your desk so as to not have eye contact with people outside. While we have all been taught about the virtues of an open door, there are times when you need to close it. Because of the fact that it is unusual, people will get the impression that you must be working on something important. Also, by shifting the direction of your desk so as to avoid direct eye contact, you will witness fewer interruptions. If people catch your

eye, they will naturally want to do the polite thing and pass the time of day.

When, a few years back, I presented a time management seminar to a group of managers at a Fortune 500 manufacturing company in Minneapolis, I mentioned this idea of closing your door and it was met with some snickering. Apparently, no one, except for the most senior of executives in this company, or at least very few people in this company, had an office door as they all worked in one of these large partitioned barns. I explained to them that when I said "close your door," I didn't necessarily mean it in the literal sense. You can do essentially the same thing by setting up a system of signals in an open-concept office. With this in mind, I presented each of the participants in attendance with a red baseball cap with our insignia on it. The plan was that whenever you wanted to, metaphorically speaking, close your door, you could simply set this hat upon your partition divider, a signal that you did not want to be interrupted at that moment in time. I later learned that while some people abused the practice by stapling their hat to the divider, most people found that it helped a great deal in reducing unnecessary drop-ins or drop-by interruptions.

4. Set up visiting hours. Try to make it known that you have a particular time of the day when you are more accepting of visitors and phone calls. Have your assistant proclaim it. If you are going to have to spend a certain amount of time interacting with your co-workers and others with legitamate and other motivations, you might as well take advantage of the principle of "chunking."

One of the best time management techniques I learned as a young, fresh-faced university professor back in the 1970s was the concept of chunking. On the first day of class, we would announce to our undergraduate students that our office hours were, say, Tuesdays and Thursdays from 9:00 a.m. until 11:00 a.m. and students were strongly advised to appear during those hours only, with or without an appointment.

The advantage of this instruction was that it allowed my colleagues and me to compress similar tasks into a common time period. You see, it is often not how much time we have to accomplish a task, but rather how much uninterrupted time we have to work on that task. Whenever someone drops in on you, even if it is only to tell you a joke that takes a minute or two, it breaks your concentration and will take you, on average, one and a half to two minutes to recover and get back to where you were. With the average manager being interrupted four times per hour, even if the interruption took just a minute, which is extremely conservative, when you add the recovery time, it amounts to somewhere around 12 minutes or 20% of your days. By slotting all student interviews into blocks of time or chunks devoted to, in this case, interviews, recovery was no longer an issue.

5. Make time for clients and customers. When it is a customer or client who drops in, you will likely want to make time for him or her. It is not unusual for customers or clients to drop in unannounced, largely because they don't feel that what they need is important enough to necessitate an appointment. If the interruption looks like it will only take a minute or two of your time, submitting will bolster the relationship you have with your customer or client. However, if what the client wants demands more time than you can afford, or he or she begins to abuse your time, politely ask him or her to come back at a time that suits you or to make an appointment.

6. Finally, if subtlety fails, you may have to just talk to them about the problem, set some boundaries, and ask for their cooperation in respecting them. Make it clear that while you value your relationship with them, you would prefer to socialize at a different time, perhaps during lunch or a coffee break.

4. The Telephone

The Telephone: We spend almost two hours per day on the telephone. For most managers, that is an average of 12-14 calls per day; for administrative professionals, it's more than double, and about 20% of that time is wasted.

The biggest problem with the telephone is that it rings!

A ringing phone has a sense of urgency to it. It's like a surprise package; you don't know what's inside until you open it. But in the case of the telephone, once you open it, it's too late—the surprise may not be something you want. By saying yes to the ringing phone, you are saying no to other more important activities. It is the break in your concentration, the interruption, that is really the problem.
Remember what we said earlier—it's not how much time you have to work on a task, it's how much uninterrupted time you have. Even if the phone call only takes one or two minutes, it will take you at least the same amount of time to recover or get back to where you were before you answered it.

As children, particularly as teenagers, the telephone was, for us, a social lifeline. It was the social tool that enabled us to be in touch and stay in touch with our friends and it offered a degree of privacy that enabled us to engage in all the social chatter and gossip that was vital to our teenage world. Now, however, the telephone has become a tool of business, an essential tool at that, designed to perform an entirely different function.

The ideal starting point is to identify how much time you are spending on the phone, when, and for what purpose. Again, this is an area for which keeping the time log I spoke about in Chapter 3 can be invaluable. You will discover that the 80/20 rule applies to the telephone. A total of 80% of your telephone interruptions are caused by 20% of the people with whom you work.

Dreamers, as you might expect, have the most difficulty in this area. The telephone provides them with an ideal opportunity to kick back and socialize. The dreamer's telephone calls tend to be longer than those of the other three because there's always a social element before and after the actual purpose of the telephone call. Supporters, on the other hand, often feel that it's rude to let a telephone ring. After all, it might be the call that relates to something important to the caller and the supporter can help him or her, or the caller may have a question that only the supporter can answer. Thinkers tend to generate a good many telephone calls seeking information and answers. It is only commanders who have little difficulty with the telephone. They do not generate a lot of outgoing calls and, when they do, their manner is businesslike and to the point.

The following suggestions may help you to deal with the telephone:

1. Screen your calls: If you're fortunate enough to have an administrative professional who can answer and screen your telephone calls, this will save you a great deal of time. You need to have prearranged, however, who always gets through, who never gets through, and when he or she can use his or her discretion.

The normal way to answer the business telephone is something like,

"Good afternoon. Mr. Smith's office. Can I help you?" This usually evokes another question, "Is he in?" Now the screening starts. Usually it's another question such as, "May I ask who's calling?" This is problematic because you've now implicitly confirmed that Mr. Smith is in. If after I announced my name, your next response is, "No I'm sorry, Mr. Douglas, he just stepped out," then it sounds a great deal like he's not in *for me*! A better question to ask may be, "Yes he is, but I'm not too sure if he's available. May I ask who's calling?" Now if the caller has a tender ego, it's not as likely to be bruised. It's vital to ask callers to identify themselves. Not only will it save the boss's time but—and this should be the case—if your administrative professional is fully apprised of, and involved with, your work and projects, he or she may be able to direct the caller to that individual within the organization who might best deal with his or her enquiry, or, at a minimum, provide you with material and information needed to better deal with that call. The assistant can also screen out those pesky investment salespeople.

If you don't have an assistant who can answer your telephone, you have just three options: you can answer it, let it ring, or have the call go to voicemail. In the absence of a human screener, the third option is the next best approach.

2. Return calls at set times: This certainly relates to the first point and takes advantage of the principle of chunking that we discussed earlier. Why not take all of your morning phone calls and begin returning them at 11:30 AM or return afternoon calls after 4. There are a couple advantages to doing this. First, you are putting like activities into a block of time, but, more importantly, since you initiated the call, proper etiquette dictates that you are able to terminate the call. Also, when calling just before lunch and closing time, people tend to get more to the point. They would rather eat lunch or go home than have a long, rambling telephone conversation with you.

---

3. Create an outline: Make a brief outline before placing an important business call. Have at hand the information or files to which you may have to refer in order to make sure that you know what it is that you're going to say. Prepare a message in case the person you're calling is no longer in and you are sent to his or her voicemail. Speak in friendly conversational tones and visualize the person to whom you're speaking.

4. Time your calls: Time your calls and keep them short and simple. A kitchen timer or egg timer can be useful in this regard. Avoid comments such as "How are you?" or "How's it going?" Have a few termination statements available, e.g., "Just one more thing before I go," or "Hey Jack, I'm not taking up a large chunk of your time but…" With chatty or long-winded callers, you may have to be even more direct, "Gina, I just can't talk now. May I call you back in a couple hours?", "Jack, I'm sorry I just had someone step into the office. I'll talk you later." I find that traffic can be a good excuse when driving. If possible, let it be known that you like to take your calls at a specified time, e.g., just before lunch or at whatever time best suits you. Have your assistant proclaim this at every opportunity.

5. Avoid telephone tag: Another time waster is telephone tag. Telephone tag is a variation of the game Ping-Pong. You receive a telephone message to return a phone call. When you do, the other person is not receiving calls and, not knowing why he or she was calling, you just state that you are returning his or her call. The original caller then calls you back but can't reach you, and so on and so on.

To avoid this, always give some indication as to what a good time would be for the individual to return your call. For example, "I'll be in the office after 2:00 p.m.." Be explicit about what it is that you need when leaving a message: "Fred, I'm trying to confirm the unit cost of the XYZ model. I need to know the unit cost and any discounts available. Please call me back. If I am not in, leave the information on my voicemail." If your call requires a much more detailed discussion, then leave a message asking what would be a good time for you to call him or her back.

Essentially, the question is: Do you control your phone, or does your phone control you?

5. Email and Internet

While originally intended as a productivity-improving, time-saving servant, for many of us, e-mail has evolved into a time-consuming, energy-sucking productivity-draining master demanding our constant attention in the office, on the road, and at home.

With our laptops, BlackBerries, iPhones, and other handheld devices, many of us find it almost impossible to escape our e-mails. Even airplanes, where, except for the motormouth in the center seat, one can usually look forward to a few hours of uninterrupted time, are increasingly providing Internet service. While e-mail has unquestionably been a great boon to the business world and our personal relationships, their nonstop transmission has become a major impairment to effective time management.

To put into context the pervasiveness of email and the problems it creates, consider the following statistics:

- *More than 90% of Internet users between 18 and 72 said they send and receive email, making it the top online activity just ahead of search engines, according to the non-profit research group. - Pew Internet and American Life Project*

- *The number of marketing emails sent by U.S. retailers and wholesalers this year will hit 158 billion and grow 63% to 258 billion in 2013. - Forrester's US Email Marketing Volume Forecast*

- *More than seven out of 10 employed respondents also said they checked their personal email at work, and nearly one-third said they did so more than three times a day. - AOL/Beta Research Corporation*

- *Nearly one-quarter of Internet users surveyed said they were most likely to check their email upon waking. - AOL/Beta Research Corporation*

- *75.8% said they are using more email than three years ago. - Direct Marketing Association*

- *Only 22% of professionals bother to unsubscribe from email they no longer want. - Return Path*

- *15% of Americans describe themselves as "addicted to email." - AOL*

- *59% of people emailing from portable devices are checking email in bed while in their pajamas; 53% in the bathroom; 37% are checking email while they drive; and 12% admit to checking email in church. - AOL*

- *Women (16%) are more likely to describe themselves as addicted to email than men (13%), and are actually spending 15 minutes more per day on email than men. - AOL*

- *Forty-three percent of email users check their email first thing in the morning, and 40% have checked their email in the middle of the night. Twenty-six percent admit to checking email on a laptop in bed while in their pajamas. - AOL*

- *Sixty percent of people who email admit to checking their personal email at work an average of three times a day. While only 15% of those who do so have been "busted" by their bosses, 28% say they feel guilty about it. - AOL*

- *Over 147 million people in the U.S. use email almost every day. - eMarketer*

- *In 2012, there are over 3,3 billion email users worldwide. - Radicati Group*

The following 10 suggestions can help you to manage your emails:

1. **Batch emails, turn off alerts:** You're working on an important project and making great headway when all of a sudden *ding!*, an e-mail alert goes off and the little picture frame pops up on your computer screen. You're afraid the e-mail may be something important. Maybe it demands a quick response. You're simply curious, so you leave the important task that you're working on then read the e-mail. Does this sound familiar? The average manager receives more than 30

e-mails per day. That's 30 times each day that you're interrupted, in most cases unnecessarily. Remember what we said before about the recovery problem; every time you're interrupted, it takes a minute and a half to two minutes to just get back to where you were. That means that on an average day, you've wasted half to three quarters of an hour just recovering or getting back to your work, rather than actually carrying out your work. This is in addition, of course, to the time you spend reading e-mails. I would suggest turning your e-mail alert off. Also, unless you're anxiously awaiting an important email that requires your immediate attention, check your e-mails at set times throughout the day, preferably no more than two or three times a day—perhaps midmorning, again after lunch, and finally, about an hour before you go home. Never check your e-mails first thing in the morning. You want to get in at least two or three hours of meaningful accomplishment before you move into reactive mode by responding to emails. This will dramatically reduce the number of times you switch tasks and activities. Statistics have shown that office workers spend 28% of their time jumping from one activity to the next because they're interrupted.

2. **Maintain a separate account for personal messages:** Create a separate account for personal e-mails and don't give your business e-mail to your friends and family nor your personal e-mail address to your colleagues or business associates. I would also recommend having a third e-mail address that you can use for requests for information, non-essential newsletters, or those occasions when you must present an email to visit a site with which you are unfamiliar or suspect may be harvesting emails for subsequent promotions.

3. **Minimize personal emails at work:** As indicated by the
    statistics above, a full 70% of business users reported
    engaging in the practice of reading personal e-mail
    correspondence during working hours. I would counsel you
    not to do so. If you must look at it, do so on your own time
    over lunch and do it using your smartphone, not the
    company's system. Some of the reasons for this are, of
    course, obvious. Doing it on the employer's dime can mean
    wasting bandwidth, etc. Some are also downright dangerous
    as they introduce viruses, worms, Trojans, and other
    malicious intruders to your employer's system. There has
    been no shortage of lawsuits and firing associated with non-
    business use of employer email and Internet resources.

4. **Create email folders:** Imagine how your office would run if
    rather than filing documents, you simply had a room with
    three huge piles of papers and documents. Well, by
    maintaining your e-mails in three folders—inbox, outbox,
    and junk—you're essentially doing the same thing. You may
    opt to create folders based on subject, project, clients,
    prospects, legal issues, etc. or simply alphabetically. But the
    point is that by having dedicated folders, your e-mails can be
    accessed more quickly and easily, and can be referred to and
    acted upon when necessary. The creation of folders is no
    more difficult than creating a folder on your laptop, and
    popular programs such as Microsoft Outlook enable you to
    do so in three or four steps.

5. **Purge and delete:** Perhaps the simplest way to control your bulging email inbox is to try to purge your insignificant e-mail messages at the end of each day and delete spam as soon as it arrives.

6. **Respond to legitimate emails quickly:** "Netiquette" suggests that we should at least acknowledge a legitimate e-mail message after we read it. This is probably a good rule, although it doesn't oblige one to take immediate action. It's just bad e-mail etiquette to ignore a legitimate e-mail message. Also, if you do ignore e-mails, their senders will continue to send messages thinking that you may have missed the first one or that it got lost in cyberspace. The best practice is simply to respond and get them out of your inbox.

7. **Fully utilize the subject line:** Most people don't use the email subject line properly. It needs to be an attention getter. Remember that part of your job as an e-mail writer is to ensure that your message is opened, read, and responded to. Make your subject line descriptive. A subject line reading, "Travel Expenses Drop by 40% this Quarter" is much more attention-grabbing than, "Travel Budget Report." Don't use your subject line to trick the reader with a misleading subject; under Canspam laws, this practice is outright illegal for marketing emails. Don't put more than one subject in your subject line and avoid the hackneyed subject lines commonly used by spammers such as "Urgent - Read Now," "Thank You," or just "Information." Recognize that many people might give your email only a cursory glance if they read it at all. For this reason, put the most important part of

your message in the subject line. For example, rather than "Planning and Review Meeting," say "Planning and Review Meeting—Tuesday 2:00 a.m."

8. **Create electronic signatures**: To save you time by reducing redundant effort, create a signature that occludes all contact information on yourself. You never know where your e-mail message might end up—perhaps on the screens of clients and coworkers, suppliers etc. Also, today it's important to have a proper use message at the bottom of every e-mail you send. The one I use on my e-mails reads as follows:

   This e-mail is confidential and is intended for the above-named recipient(s) only. If you are not the intended recipient, please notify us by telephone or return e-mail immediately and delete this e-mail from your system without making a copy. Any unauthorized use or disclosure of this e-mail is prohibited.

9. **Deal with spam proactively:** Avoid posting your e-mail address on public message boards or newsgroups as spammers routinely harvest e-mails from these sites. I would also recommend not using Hotmail, Gmail, Yahoo, or MSN as your primary mail provider as spammers typically flood these with obvious possible usernames (paul123, paul12, paul1957, etc.) I would think twice about printing your e-mail address on letterheads and business cards. Don't reply to spam or click the unsubscribe link. Most spammers will not respect your request; in fact, it simply confirms to them that you're a live prospect for future spam. It also motivates the spammer to sell your address to others. I would also be

careful about subscribing to online newsletters without checking the publisher's privacy policy. Most major organizations today have invested in sophisticated and effective anti-spam software programs, but if yours has not done so then get your own, and certainly install a good anti-spam program on your personal laptop or home computer. Of course, it goes without saying that you should not click on the link embedded in an e-mail from a stranger; in fact, I would not open an e-mail from an unknown sender, particularly if the subject line is suspect or contains odd characters or unusual spelling as spammers often use these techniques in order to frustrate anti-spam software. You might also consider using the auto preview option available on Microsoft Outlook and other popular e-mail programs; these enable you to look at a few lines of the message without actually opening it.

10. **Don't BIF people afterhours:** "BIF," which stands for "before I forget," is often used to refer to e-mails sent outside of normal work hours—evenings and weekends. It comes from your fear of forgetting to do something or following up in a timely manner. This has the effect of creating a 24/7 workday expectation. If you think of something that you should send to your assistant while you're watching the late show on Saturday night, don't send her an e-mail; simply scribble a note down in your datebook organizer or put it in your iPhone or BlackBerry for Monday.

6. Paperwork

We spoke briefly earlier about reducing clutter by sorting through all the papers that we accumulated and saving, forwarding, or filing what we were unable to toss. Having done so, it's important to now deal more effectively with the paperwork that we are generating and that comes in our direction so that we don't put ourselves back into that disorganized bind once again.

I've heard supposed time management experts say repeatedly that we should handle paper only once. I think it's important not to keep picking up, reviewing, and re-stacking paper, but I believe once is probably unrealistic—twice maybe. I think that if we apply our four criteria as we handle each piece of paper for the first time— "action," "pending," "pass on," or "filing"—this will reduce the amount of paper that is stacked and uncategorized. If it's a request for information that you can scribble across the bottom of this letter or memo and mail back, or if it's something you can respond to by e-mail briefly or by picking up the phone and making a short call, then do so now and immediately. I had a small stamp made up that read, "Please excuse the cursive nature of this response, but I thought you would prefer speed to formality. - Paul Douglas."

But if, and this is often the case, your response requires greater thought, information, or data, in other words more time, then put it in the "pending" file. Thinkers beware, however; be sure that you are not putting items in the "pending" file because you need more information; rather, it should be done because you are unable or unwilling to make an immediate decision.

If it is something that a member of your team needs to have, drop it in the "pass on" file; otherwise, discard it.

I would encourage you to use dictation equipment in order to more efficiently deal with correspondence. While, at first, this may seem foreign, it will save you an incredible amount of time provided you learn to use the equipment properly. It's best to first write an outline of what you are hoping to say. Scribble it down in point form. Remember, too, that when people do transition to the dictation system, their letters and memos tend to be much longer than they normally would be insofar as we speak in conversational terms. Keep brevity in mind as you dictate. If you're answering a letter with a number of questions that need to be addressed, respond to them by number and in order—a paragraph in response to each of their questions, even if it's only one sentence. Dictate as quickly as possible and don't strive for perfection; your conversational voice is better than you think and you can go back and clean it up on the final document.

Again, this is an area where the new technology really needs to be looked at. There have been incredible advances in the last few years. If you don't have an assistant who can create your correspondence from your dictations, purchase a voice recognition software package. At the time of writing, Dragon Dictation® for either Mac® or PC is, in my opinion, the finest software out there. It quickly learns the unique aspects of your speech and provides instant spelling and grammar checking. Another product produced by Nuance, called MacSpeech Scribe®, enables you to download voice recordings and create written copy from your smartphone or handheld recorder.

By switching from keyboarding or written drafts to electronic dictation, the average manager can reduce the time spent dealing with correspondence and other written material by 50%. That is a major source of new time.

Filing: What Thinkers Love and Dreamers Hate

When you have finally pared things down to what you really need to keep, you need to put them in a place where you can find them, and in an office environment, this means a filing system.

First, recognize the difference between working files and archival material—temporary (working) and permanent (archival).

Determining when and how often a file will be used should tell you which type it is.

Temporary files include:

1. Your action file
2. Project plans, documents, and notes related to current projects
3. Your reading file

Permanent files include:

- Documents you originated.
- Documents that may contribute to future projects or relationships
- Material for which retention is required for legal or regulatory reasons.

There is no one best filing system. The important thing is to ensure that it suits your personality and supports your objectives. It must be simple yet effective. The test of a good filing system is this: can you find a document or receipt from two years ago, within three minutes?

A filing system doesn't have to be complicated to be effective; in fact, the opposite is true. Keep it simple. Arrange files alphabetically by subject using nouns, and label files according to the broadest generic headings that are meaningful to you—training, prospects, newsletters, etc. Arrange documents within each folder chronologically back to front, i.e., the most recent addition to the file is placed at the front. Receipts should be filed the same way.

On the outside of the file, write the date on which you created the file. This can be useful when it comes to purging your files in the future.

Think about color-coding—all tax files are red, all HR employee files are blue, all client files are green, etc.

Recently, in my own office, we purchased a high-speed document scanner by Neat®. It has OCR and parsing technology that can read and extract key information from a document or receipt. Not only can it recognize the difference between a document, business card, or receipt, and automatically place it in the appropriate document file, remarkably, it does the same with receipts, even keeping a running total for each expense category.

Duck: Incoming

If you are serious about improving your efficiency when it comes to paperwork, it is important to stem the flow. Ask people if reports they prepare, or for that matter that you prepare, are really necessary. Prepare them only if and when needed. Reduce the number of memos you keep. Remember, memos are primarily for short-term information.

Throw out last month's copy of a magazine when the current month's copy arrives, and, of course, cancel subscriptions to magazines and newspapers that you no longer read. Reduce the number of credit cards you carry as this reduces the number of statements as well as bill-paying time. If you find yourself dealing with multiple bank statements every month, reduce the number of accounts you have and pay your bills by automatic deduction where possible. These are a few places where you can start.

7. Meetings

We live in a democracy. We accept, almost as an article of faith, that our country, company, church, and even family will work better if we choose together what needs to be done and how we need to do it.

We are surrounded by examples of individuals coming together to plan, share information, make decisions, and solve problems. Everywhere today, people are having meetings. Great things come out of meetings—the Magna Carta, Declaration of Independence, and the Last Supper.

We have meetings for many different reasons—to inform, to analyze and solve problems, to discuss and exchange views, to inspire and motivate, to persuade, to train and develop, or to instigate change. Meetings keep people informed and up to date and provide an opportunity to be heard. They also provide visibility and an opportunity for personal public relations and can broaden an individual's experience and provide a learning opportunity. However, the most important reason for meetings is to make decisions.

I often conduct an exercise at my management seminars that requires those in attendance to picture themselves as members of a mountain-climbing expedition attempting to climb Mt. Robson, the highest peak in the Canadian Rockies. They are informed that due to a disastrous avalanche, half of their climbing team is swept away. It, therefore, falls on one member of the survivors to travel down to base camp to get help. The team's life depends on it.

The participants are told that they have been chosen and that they have to move quickly and lightly. They, therefore, can choose only 13 of 35 items to take with them to help get them down the mountain. They can choose from among items such as a pickaxe, matches, oxygen, sleeping bag, thermos of coffee, etc. When everyone has made his or her selection, we then break them into small groups and ask them to reach a consensus on what the group thinks are the best choices. Finally, I reveal what the Alpine Club of Canada, the experts, say are the 13 most important items.

We then have both the individuals and the groups compare their choices against the experts' list and calculate their error scores.

Having led this exercise for at least 20 years, I must tell you that there has never been one occasion when the individual averages were higher than the group averages. In other words, the groups, on average, make better decisions than do the individuals. Yes, there may have been one or two individuals who made a better selection than the best group, but, on average, they didn't fare as well.

This is really why we have meetings—because better and safer decisions come out of them. When it comes to decision making, two minds are better than one and, of course, twelve are better than two.

But not all meetings are effective, although they are always costly. The typical manager spends around 15 hours a week in meetings and another six hours getting ready for those meetings. Also, it has been estimated that 25%–35% of that time is wasted. That works out to be over a full month of squandered time each year.

The Cost of Meetings

Most organizations do not realize the real cost of their meetings. Often when I point out to my clients the cost of their weekly meetings, they are surprised and shocked.

There are two ways to count the costs of meetings. The first is to simply take the approximate salaries of each of the participants in attendance and divide this by 1,800 hours, the number of hours the average person works each year. Then add 30% for overhead (health care, retirement plans, etc.) and multiply this by the number of participants and the length of the meeting in hours or the fractions thereof.

For example, if you have 14 managers with an average salary of $80,000 meeting for two hours, this will cost the organization $1,617. Had the group been senior executives, that meeting could have cost $10,000 or more, and this doesn't take into consideration travel time or refreshments.

The second way to calculate the cost of meetings is to take the annual sales or budget of an organization, divide this by the number of employees in that organization, then divide the product by 1,800 and add 30%.

For example if your annual sales are $100 million and you have 1,200 employees, then, on average, each employee brings $83,000 to the organization. Divide this by 1,800 and add 30% and you have the value of each employee's time being $60.19 per hour. The chart below illustrates this calculation for a few organizations:

Here are some of the common reasons why so much time is wasted in meetings:

- **Too many**
- **No real purpose**
- **No agenda**
- **Agenda not adhered to**
- **Lack of preparation**
- **Too many/wrong people present**
- **Don't start on time**
- **Don't end on time**
- **No results or decisions**
- **Poor follow-up**

There are a number of ways in which we can improve our meetings:

The first question you should ask is, "Do we need this meeting in the first place?" Consider other alternatives. Don't call a meeting. If it's a matter for debate or consultation, ask yourself if the information can be circulated in some other way—telephone calls, email blasts, memos, etc. Remember the costs involved in holding a meeting. If you're at all unsure, then don't call the meeting.

The objectives for the meeting should be clearly stated and each individual in attendance should be fully aware of why we are meeting. This presupposes that many meetings are held every day without any real or stated purpose. The objectives should be discussed in behavioral terms—"To decide how to reduce our travel budget by 20% over the next 12 months," not "To discuss the travel budget."

Always have a clear meeting plan. It's important to produce this plan or agenda and distribute it to each participant at least 24 hours before the meeting. One of the reasons why so many items are carried over to the agenda for the next meeting is that individuals have not had an opportunity to think about the issues being considered and simply don't feel comfortable enough making the relevant decisions without proper thought. Also, if you create an agenda, stick to it. Discourage dealing with items under "other business." In fact, I would recommend not having a section on the agenda called "other business" as it only encourages people to surface their pet projects without giving attendees a chance to think about the issues arising from them in advance.

The agenda should communicate the purpose of the meeting. Is it to solve a short-term tactical problem, or a critical long-term strategic issue? Are participants meant to discuss and debate, offer alternatives, or just sit and listen? Try not to confuse people by letting the meeting devolve into a combination of all of the above.

A good agenda will indicate the order in which items will be dealt with and will identify the specific results to be achieved for each agenda item. It will also deal with all administrative matters—time and venue, for example. It will also indicate any formalities required—visual aids needed etc.

Prepare the room. Have everything required in the room. There's nothing more aggravating than a roomful of highly paid executives sitting around waiting for someone to locate a blackboard eraser or remote for the overhead projector.

Don't make people too comfortable. As a young consultant, I recalled being invited to a number of board meetings at a very successful oil company in Calgary, Canada. These meetings were held in the top-floor boardroom of a skyscraper in downtown Calgary with a magnificent view of the Canadian Rockies. We sat around a boardroom table made of African blackwood, reportedly imported at a cost of $200,000. The chairs on which we sat were ergonomically designed, and we were served gourmet sandwiches and every beverage you could imagine, by attractive young women. We never wanted these meetings to end! Going to one of these meetings was like a trip back to the womb. Perhaps not surprisingly, that company is, incidentally, no longer in business.

I am not advocating stand-up meetings by the comestibles, and surroundings should not distract from the task at hand.

Think about banning all cell phones, BlackBerries and other communication devices from your meetings. They are distractions for both their owners and those around them.

I've been a licensed pilot for well over 40 years now and became familiar with a term in the aviation community known as "sterile cockpit." It's actually an FAA cockpit rule that reads, "Activities such as eating meals, engaging in nonessential conversations within the cockpit and nonessential communications between the cabin and the cockpit crew and reading publications not related to the proper conduct of the flight are not required for the safe operation of the aircraft." This rule exists so that at critical junctions in the flight— takeoff and landing— the pilots of the aircraft do not become preoccupied with anything unrelated to the most important task at hand. As much as possible, I would recommend that you promote this type of "sterile cockpit" thinking in your meetings.

Allow people to come and go as their conscious individual contribution is required and completed.

Start the meeting on time even if the CEO has not shown up. If people quickly learn that their meetings always start 10 minutes late, they will start appearing at least 10 minutes late as well. It's also unfair to punish those individuals who are well organized and do show up on time. Give thought to when the meeting should be held and try to schedule it at such a time—usually in the morning—when most participants will be at their most alert and perhaps most creative. I would also recommend not setting an end time for the meeting where possible. If you tell people that the planning and review meeting will be between 9:00 a.m. and 11:00 a.m. on Wednesday morning, you'll seldom get out of the room before 11:00 am. Parkinson's law—which states that activities will expand much like in a bottle to fill the space available for their completion—then takes over. If people are told that they have half an hour, they will often get it done in half an hour.

If these types of structural changes are beyond your control, then for goodness' sake, end the damn thing on time!

Deal with the most important things first.

Choose your participants carefully. Try to assemble the correct group to match their expertise to the topic being discussed and avoid inviting people because of their organizational status or for political or social reasons. If they have nothing meaningful to contribute to the meeting, they shouldn't be there. Remember that each additional person in attendance will lengthen your meeting.

Each meeting should always have a chairperson and a secretary. The chairperson leads the meeting and the secretary records and takes the minutes.

Choose your chairperson carefully. You want someone strong enough to keep the long-winded quiet and the silent involved. Watch for the person to whom most team members look when speaking. This is the natural chair, even though he or she may not be the highest ranking. This person should be at the tiller.

Close your meeting by summarizing what was and was not accomplished and, finally, prepare a follow-up or action plan detailing what needs to be done, who needs to do it, and when it needs to be done.

8. Delegation

Delegation is the assignment of a specific task or project to another person, as well as the acceptance of, and commitment to, that assignment by that other person. Effective delegation requires not only the transfer of work, but also of accountability for the project and sufficient authority to successfully accomplish it. You can delegate authority, accountability, or both. What delegation does not do is remove the ultimate responsibility for the successful completion of the task or project. That is, and will remain, yours. Delegation is simply getting work done through others.

Delegation is one of the most important skills in a manager's repertoire. It is vital to effective leadership, and yet it's one of the most difficult things to teach. Good delegation will not only motivate and develop the people around you, it will reduce your workload and free up additional time for you. This time can lead to greater success in your life as you focus on other, more important priorities. Poor delegation, on the other hand, will not only reduce your personal productivity, but will lead to resentment and a lowering of morale on the part of your staff.

There are many other benefits of successful delegation.

Benefits of Delegation

- It frees up time that can be used on more productive things

- It enables or develops staff growth by expanding their knowledge base

- It increases trust and cooperation within your team

- It increases motivation and the overall level of morale

- It serves your organization by having the right person doing the right job

- It enhances your teaching and coaching skills and abilities.

We've all heard the expression, "It takes money to make money." The same might be said of delegation—"It takes time to save time." When I speak with managers who are having difficulty delegating, the most common reason or excuse I hear is, "It would take me longer to explain to that person how to do it to my standards, than it would for me to do it myself. I simply don't have that kind of time right now." They are taking the short-term perspective, whereas delegation requires a long-term perspective.

There are a number of warning signs that your delegation skills are lacking. These include the following:

Symptoms of Poor Delegation

- Your in-basket is overflowing.

- You are taking work home or working late to complete tasks that "only you can do."

- Your staff seems to lack initiative.

- There is low morale or high staff turnover.

- You often feel as if you are buried in trivia.

- You often intervene in assignments that you have given to others.

- Deadlines are missed.

- You feel overworked.

Effective delegation isn't just a matter of telling someone else to do something. There are several levels of delegation:

1. Delegate part of the task

2. Delegate all of the task.

3. Delegate the work but retain the decision-making authority.

4. Delegate work and decision making but expect frequent progress reports.

5. Delegate everything and ask for results at the end.

Effective delegation empowers others. It gives those people charged with accomplishing a task enough authority to get on with it without constantly having to look above for approval and permission. Team members often feel undervalued and underutilized. They do the work assigned competently enough but often seek a chance to prove what they are really capable of. The situation can breed boredom and discontent. By giving your staff greater responsibility, you will benefit further by their increased level of commitment.

As a general rule, work should be delegated to the person at the lowest pay grade who is capable of accomplishing the task. The important thing here, of course, is that the delegate is capable of completing the assignment successfully. More time can be spent trying to rectify a problem than completing the task in the first place.

Wherever possible, delegation should be established as a routine matter. It should not look like you're asking a subordinate for a favor. If delegation is routine, staff members are more likely to accept and complete assignments. Also, of course, care should be taken to delegate work evenly among all staff members.

Organizational Economics

A British economist by the name of David Ricardo spoke of the **Law of Comparative Advantage**. This law, referring to world trade, held that all nations would benefit by manufacturing those goods that they could produce most efficiently, and importing those goods that other countries could produce at an acceptable level of quality and value at a lower cost. He was able to demonstrate mathematically that even though a country such as Spain, for example, could produce two products, say grapes and oranges, at a higher level of quality than, say, Portugal, it was still better for Spain to concentrate exclusively on producing the one product that it made best—oranges—and letting Portugal produce grapes for export to Spain. Ricardo was able to show that, under this protocol, total utility increased for both nations.

This law or rule also applies to organizational life. The organization benefits when its participants concentrate on those tasks and those areas in which they have a comparative advantage. The law of comparative advantage would say that, for example, if you are a junior executive making $150,000 a year, or approximately $85 per hour, you should hire someone to do any jobs that can be done for a rate of $85 per hour or less. If you are a lawyer billing $300 per hour and you can find a paralegal to do some of your work—conveyancing, for example, for a wage of $40 per hour—it would be wise to do so. Delegation allows us to direct work downward toward lower-paid staff rather than higher-paid managers.

What to Delegate

There are four categories of tasks that are good candidates for delegation.

Routine: Tasks that you perform repeatedly are good candidates for delegation because they're very easy to pass on to a subordinate. Because you've done them repeatedly, you're well aware of any problems or pitfalls that may arise and you've no doubt developed efficient procedures for accomplishment. Opening the mail, paying bills, filing, boilerplate responses to requests for information, etc.

would fall under this category.

Trivia: It's very easy for busy managers or executives to become involved in matters way below their pay scale—activities that, in the long run, have very little to do with what it is they are hoping to achieve. These types of trivial pursuits become ideal targets for delegation. Try to resist your natural tendency to say, "It's not worth delegating." It really is. If you can't eliminate it altogether, delegate it.

Necessities: These are the things that must be done. They may be demands made by your boss or they may involve decisions that require very little managerial judgment, for example, reviewing sales figures or reconciling budgets.

Specialties: This comes back to the law of comparative advantage. We should delegate when we lack the level of knowledge or expertise necessary to perform a particular task and when we have no interest in acquiring that skill set. Hiring an accountant to do your tax return would be an example of this. Can you do your own tax return? Sure you can! But in order to do it properly, you're going to have to develop some ability that you don't currently have, and, without question, you're going to be much more inefficient in the completion of performance schedules than an experienced account would be.

What NOT to Delegate

There are also four areas that you should not seek to delegate:

Policy: As managers, we should not delegate responsibilities that require the determination of policy because policy sets the limits of decision making. If, for example, a manager were to delegate to his assistants the task of interviewing candidates for the position of IT specialist, he might delegate all of the screening functions to his assistants based on criteria that he had determined. The manager, however, retains ultimate responsibility for the decision as to who to hire. This is good and altogether appropriate delegation. If, however, the manager instructed his assistants to set their own criteria for hiring, then he's gone too far. If his assistants made a decision based on a criterion they developed that included racial or gender bias, it would be the manager who would be responsible for this improper action. Additionally, of course, we never delegate the overall leadership of the group.

Ritual: The second area of responsibility that should not be delegated is ritual. This comprises activities and responsibilities that fall on you as a result of your position, not your skills. This, for example, is why when there's a major oil spill, it is the president of that organization who responds to the media. Often, the president is neither the most knowledgeable nor is he or she necessarily most aware of the issues or, for that matter, the most skillful when it comes to dealing with the media—but it is ritual. Speaking at the retirement dinner of a longtime employee or delivering condolences would likewise fall under this category.

Sensitive personnel matters: The appraisal and employee evaluation of staff members reporting to the manager would fall under this category, as well as any disciplinary action involving one of these employees or delivering acknowledge and praise to them. Resolving conflicts between staff members is also the responsibility of the manager.

Confidential matters: All organizations have secrets, situations, and information of which management, but no one else, is aware. It might relate to salaries, security matters, or personal indiscretions committed by staff members. Matters of this kind, even though they hardly require the manager's skill set, must be handled personally by him or her.

How to Delegate

A proven system for improving the "how to" of delegation is the adherence to the five steps, techniques, and rules indicated by the SMART acronym. It is my guess that you might have heard of this before. It's one of the worst-kept secrets of effective time management techniques.

S – Specific: We need to be specific with regard to the end result that we are seeking. It's essential to provide delegatees with the details and full scope of the project, letting them know what you want them to end up with and why. By being specific in this regard, delegates will understand precisely what it is that they need to do, as well as the reasons for its importance.

M – Measurable: It's important that we make the assignments quantifiable. It's only by knowing specifically what the detailed results look like that the delegatee will know when they have been achieved. This may involve setting milestones along the way. Spell out the way the delegatee will be judged.

A – Agreed: "A" stands for agreed. It's essential that you have "buy in" on the part of the delegate. This implies that you make yourself available to that person to answer questions and explain the reasons and rationales for the task itself. When giving an assignment to another person, the why is as important as the what. Agree on a deadline for completion as well as a review time—and don't hover. If you give an assignment on Monday that has a due date of Friday, then you may want to set up a review for Wednesday. This will give time to make adjustments and ensure that the task is successfully accomplished.

R – Realistic: It's important to make both the scope of the assignment and the deadline for its completion realistic. To do otherwise is to set your team member up for failure. Seek feedback along the way with regard to feasibility. Also be realistic; don't ask people to do what they cannot do. Try to link the task to the person with the appropriate skill set and knowledge level. Remember to take into account practical constraints; for example, assigning to many tasks to one person is viewed as unfair.

T – Timely: Always put a deadline on each assignment and, if a review time is involved, set a specific time for that as well. If you don't, people will procrastinate. If you say "If you get a chance, would you send a copy of our planning report off to Mary?" then don't count on Mary getting it soon because you have not set a deadline, there is no apparent urgency, and the understanding is that it can be delivered at any time in the indefinite future.

In order to convey some urgency, you MUST put a deadline on tasks.

Having done so, try to then manage by exception; that is, if the project is on track and on schedule, then the delegate does not have to report back to you. "T" could also stand for "thank you." It's important to show your appreciation. This is often overlooked but when you do show sincere appreciation to the delegate for the successful completion of a project in time and within budget, you will be much more likely to see that person accept and complete other projects in the future.

9. Perfectionism

Scratch the surface of any thinker and you'll find a perfectionist. Thinkers only have one way of doing something and that's perfectly. While in many ways this is laudable, it can have a negative impact on both the organization and the perfectionists themselves. Perfectionism is a form of neurotic behavior, an irrational belief that says that you and your environment must be perfect. It's more than striving for excellence; it's more than trying to do your best; it's setting the bar so high that excellence becomes average and average becomes failure.

The driver "be perfect" can often be traced to one's youth and childhood. Overly critical parents or teachers, a rigid moralistic outlook, and punishing weakness and failure may contribute to it, although there is some evidence that would suggest that a demanding, self-critical, and perfectionistic personality is, to a large degree, independent of nurturing.

Fear of failure and fear of rejection are clearly associated with it.

Perfectionism dictates that there is no sense in trying to accomplish something unless you can do it perfectly. This driver says that you are of no value and are undeserving of love if you fail—just another loser.

The negative consequences associated with perfectionism are numerous and serious. Obviously, feelings of low self-worth and self-esteem, never feeling that you're good enough, result in a lack of confidence or the feeling that you cannot face the world as it presents itself to you each day. Guilt in the form of shame and even self-loathing may be witnessed.

Also, applying your perfectionistic standards to your mate and others can be highly destructive to your relationships. Although it often backfires, perfectionists attempt to pass this mindset on to their children.

This irrational belief that you must be perfect in everything that you undertake and the inevitable realization that you're not a perfect being can lead to depression; addictive, compulsive behaviors; and over-indulgence in alcohol, drugs, gambling, and sex, all of which are often used to medicate the perfectionist.

In terms of the scope of this book, perfectionism impacts effective time management in several ways. It often results in procrastination. Perfectionists will often fear that they can't do everything perfectly and this can be immobilizing. They will put off decisions and actions until such time that they have all of the information and data available so that they can do a perfect job. The difficulty is that they are never in possession of all the data out there.

Their behavior also results in the failure to delegate as they believe that no one else can do the job as well as they can since no one else can meet their standards.

Like "Type A" behavior, it is very difficult to alter. You are essentially required to change your outlook on life—to learn to accept yourself as an imperfect but human being, to forgive yourself for mistakes and failings, and to set realistic time frames for the accomplishment of goals and projects.

Sometimes a life-changing event is needed, such as a near-death experience or the loss of a loved one. But sometimes—and I hope that's the case here—education and self-examination are enough to move one in the right direction.

Try to associate, particularly in the workplace, with people who do not have perfectionistic tendencies.

Perfectionists often value each task or project equally and have difficulty assigning priorities to tasks and projects. I can remember a training seminar that I was leading, where I talked about "to do" lists and setting priorities. A three-star general commented that everything he did was important. Even if this was true and not his ego speaking, it was irrelevant. It's not about how important a task is, it's about how important that task is in relation to the other tasks that one hopes to accomplish.

It comes down to better planning and prioritization; this is essential. Take a little extra time at the beginning to set your priorities and re-examine your goals in order to ensure that are they realistic and attainable.

If you find yourself procrastinating when it comes to an important task or project because it's so daunting, break it down into smaller pieces. Use the "Swiss cheese" approach; Swiss is the cheese with all the holes in it. Gnaw a little hole in it here and a little hole in it there and before you know it, you have it to a size where you can gobble it all up.

"Good enough" is a satisfactory standard for a lot of the work that we do, but not for everything that we do. In most cases, there's not much difference between 99 and 100%. A major league pitcher is considered brilliant if he can hit three out of every 10 pitches.

Try to delegate more and stop yourself from constantly asking for progress reports.

10. Inability to Say "NO"

Unquestionably, the greatest time management problem that supporters have is the inability to say no.

We all want other people to like us. Every human being wants the respect, acceptance, and maybe even the admiration of others. And we all understand that as a member of an organization, a company, a church, community group, or even a family, in return for the benefits we receive through our membership, we have to share a certain amount of our time with others. But sometimes the demands placed on us by other people are in direct conflict with our own needs and priorities. It is at these times that we have to have the ability to say "no." Most of us have been in a position where our boss or a colleague or customer has asked us to do something that is clearly counter to our goals and objectives and counterproductive in terms of the use of our time.

Not everyone has a problem with this. Not all the behavioral styles find it difficult to say no. Commanders, for example, have very little difficulty. When they receive a request from another, they instantly enter into a WIIFM cost-benefit analysis asking, "What's in it for me?" Dreamers, on the other hand, are assertive individuals who have no difficulty saying "no" but often fail to do so because they fear that doing so means a lost opportunity—that they have closed a door or burned a bridge.

On the other end of the continuum, however, we have supporters, who want everyone to succeed, to be happy, and to experience high levels of self-esteem. They do not want to disappoint and often sacrifice their own needs or goals to help others to accomplish theirs. This is not always done happily; sometimes they experience feelings of resentment, but nonetheless they too often say yes rather than no.

Supporters are kindhearted, agreeable individuals who honestly want to help other people. They dislike conflict and seek to avoid it whenever possible. They fear that conflict might lead to rejection or even an ugly confrontation. They also don't wish to appear rude. If you nodded to any of these reasons, you're not alone, but I can tell you that saying no is not rude nor does it mean that you are a disagreeable person. If for no other reason than self-preservation, you have to learn how to say "no" and to do so without feeling guilty.

Learning to say "no" more effectively is a "zero sum game." Every time you say "yes" to one thing, you're really saying "no" to something else. When you say "yes" to working overtime, you're saying "no" to your social and family life. When you say "yes" to a job that you dislike, you're saying "no" to your dreams, and when you say "yes" to something you hate, you're saying "no" to something that you might love.

The following are eight suggestions for saying "no" that are practical and doable for all of the behavioral styles, including the supporter.

1. Keep it short and sweet: Let them know you can't do it by providing a short explanation: "I have other priorities at the moment," or "John, my plate is so full I can't. Perhaps next time."

There's no reason to give long, elaborate apologies and explanations and, in fact, to do so is risky because the person making the request may find a chink in your armor. When asked, for example, by a boss to work overtime on short notice, if your response is, "I wish I could but I have to pick up my son from hockey at 7:30," there's a real danger that by providing so much information, your boss may find a solution that takes care of your son's retrieval from hockey while also allowing him to ensure that his own needs are met.

In sales training, this is called dealing with objections. If, for example, you want to be a life insurance salesperson, the first thing they are going to do is teach you how to overcome the objections people have to buying life insurance;—the most common reasons or excuses people will give. Regardless of the goods or services you are trying to sell, there are certain objectives which the veterans in your particular sales field are familiar with and have learned to overcome. In the case of life insurance, it might be, "I'm sorry, I have all the life insurance I need," or "I don't believe in life insurance," "or "I can't afford life insurance." If you respond to a request to buy with an objection, you provide the salesperson with an in; They will try to overcome your objection. In the case of life insurance, their response might be to talk about budget plans, "Well can you afford $2 a day?"

2. Provide an alternative whenever possible. If you're unable or unwilling to do what's being requested or feel that you're not the right person to satisfy the request, try to provide an alternative: "I just can't look at it now. But I know Janet is very knowledgeable in that area and has had some success with it in the past." Focusing on the other person's goal rather than the course of action required will help you to come up with alternative options that may help. But remember, this is simply an act of goodwill; don't overcompensate by taking responsibility for the individual's request.

3. Try saying "Yes...but." Over the past forty years, I have worked with over 100,000 administrative professionals at my seminars and workshops and I know how difficult saying "no" to a boss can be. I'm often asked, "How do I respond to a boss who asks me to do a personal favor or run a personal errand that I really don't want to do?" My advice to that person is "Try saying 'yes, but...'" To a boss who says something like, "Janet, you know my son's in university this year and needs a term paper typed. He's so disorganized and has no keyboarding skills. Could you type this term paper out for him?" My advice is to respond with something like, "SURE! I'd be happy to! BUT is it okay then if the Anderson file waits until Monday?" What you are likely to find out pretty quickly is that, no, it's not okay! The important, work-related Anderson report can't wait until Monday. Your boss was hoping that you would type his son's paper in addition to the Anderson file, not instead of it. But this response at least puts you in a negotiating posture. You appear compliant but have placed the request back in your boss's court, forcing him to decide between the two activities. This technique works best when you can couple it with the second recommendation above—providing an alternative. In this instance, you might want to talk about typing services that can do the typing project quickly for a nominal cost of $5 or $10 per page.

Another variation on this is the quid pro quo, which says essentially I'll do this for you if you do this for me. "Jack, I don't mind working overtime again tonight, but I'll need a day off next week in order to catch up on everything at home."

4. Delay your response. I'm not suggesting for a moment here that you say "maybe." By saying something like "Let me think about that and get back to you," you run the danger of this being interpreted as a tentative yes. What I am suggesting is that if you are unable to come up with an appropriate response off the top your head, give yourself time to think of one. "Jack, I am rushing to a meeting. Let me look at it and I'll get back to you before lunch."

But don't be a waffler. Waffling misleads others because it suggests to them that you are still considering it when, in fact, you have already decided that it is a "no." It is certainly dishonest and unethical.

Supporters may be the worst at this but it is certainly not indicative of their style alone.

Waffling is driven by a desire to avoid any interpersonal conflict. It is when someone says to a salesperson something like, "No, this is perfect. Let me just speak with my partner and I'll get back to you," despite having already decided that he or she can't afford it or prefers another product. It is when, at the end of a lackluster date, you say to that person, "I'll call you," knowing fully that you won't. Stop waffling; make a decision. Summon the courage to be firm and direct with others.

5. Seek clarification if unsure. First, seek clarification if you are at all unsure as to the nature or scope of what is being requested. Most of us have had the experience of committing ourselves to what we thought was a small task or favor, only to discover, unhappily and too late, that its completion is tantamount to building a pyramid! They failed to describe all the background and research needed for completion of the request. If you suspect this to be the case, or if the person making the request has a history, seek clarification before you commit yourself one way or the other. Don't buy a pig in a poke.

6. Become the broken record. Most reasonable people will accept your refusal with good grace—but not everyone will. Some people simply can't take no for an answer. They almost take it as a personal challenge to try to get you to change your mind.

I learn a lot at airports. Not too long ago, I was waiting to catch a flight in Las Vegas and I happened to notice a well-dressed woman with a small child, a little boy, who looked to be about five or six, sitting nearby. This bright young child happened to notice a large toy airplane hanging in a nearby shop. I could hear him ask his mother, "Mommy can I have that airplane?" pointing to the toy. His mother responded kindly, "No it's too big, and we'll be boarding in a minute. Read your book." Not to be deterred, the child repeated, "Mommy, can I have the airplane?" This time, the mother responded, "No, Johnny, I told you. We haven't got time." Again, "Mommy, can I have the airplane?" This must've gone on for about 10 minutes when suddenly the woman jumped to her feet, grabbed the child by his hand, literally dragged him into the toy store, and bought the airplane. I thought to myself, "Lady, what have you just taught that child?" He just learned that you have to push that button sixteen times to get your way. God help her when he's a teenager!

If you find yourself being confronted with people of this ilk, introduce the nag to the broken record. You simply say "no," and whatever other reason or explanation you had given, like the little boy wanting the airplane, using the exact same words each time. "No, John, I just can't sit on the committee this year because of other commitments." "No John, I just can't sit on the committee this year because of other commitments." Always start with the word "no" and repeat it as often as is necessary. Eventually, even the most persistent nag will give in and give up.

7. Actually use the word "NO." The word "no" is one of the only words in the English language that lacks ambiguity. It's also one of the first words that we learn as a child when we go to touch a hot stove or wander off.. For that reason, weave the word "no" into your conversation. Make it the first word in your refusal: "No, John,

I just can't sit on the committee this year because of other commitments."

8. End on a positive note. Try to wrap up your "no" conversation on a positive note. No matter what technique you employ, make it clear that you are saying "no" to the request, not the person. Be diplomatic; say no with a smile. Most people will accept and forgive a refusal if it is done with a pleasant manner and a smile. A smile communicates to the person that you still like him or her. I have found that this smile also works on the telephone. Your smile travels down the line.

Also, don't make the common mistake of attacking the project as being flawed, unfeasible, or without value in order to justify your refusal, e.g., "John, you know this is a total waste of time." But be clear in your communication; make "yes" mean "yes" and "no" mean "no."

11. Focus and Forgetfulness

Do you live in the moment? Or do you spend your life worrying about tomorrow or being saddened by the past? Are you paying attention to one thing at a time or to a dozen?

Successful time management starts with the ability to concentrate and focus your attention singly on the task at hand. By honing your concentration down to a laser-like focus, you will create an energy that will enable you to accomplish much in a very short period of time.

If, on the other hand, your concentration is scattered, and you spend your day jumping from one task and responsibility to another, this energy will be dissipated and you will experience feelings of frustration rather than satisfaction.

Focus, then, is the ability to concentrate single-mindedly on the task at hand without allowing interruptions and other distractions to alter your course. If you can learn to improve your ability to concentrate and focus, you would get much more done and would be able to go home at night with feelings of satisfaction rather than frustration.

Focus is essential to success. Anything that reduces your focus reduces your effectiveness. Multitaskers, like dreamers, typically don't understand this. They jump from one activity to another, simultaneously balancing a number of tasks and projects. They suffer from what the Zen Buddhists call "Monkey Mind," travelling through the jungle, leaping from vine to vine while allowing their minds to jump from one task to the next.

Because they are busy and active, even frenetic, they think that they are accomplishing a great deal. This is, in reality, rarely the case. The research clearly shows that multitaskers get less done than those who focus or concentrate on one activity at a time. Studies have shown, for example, that students do worse on their homework when they multitask. There is a noticeable drop-off in their efficiency. We need to increase our focus and concentration.

Have you ever received an email from your boss or a colleague asking about a task you were supposed to be working on, but you forgot about and hadn't yet started? Or promised your boss you would take care of something important but forgot to do it? Have you missed important meetings?

A good memory is not just an absolute necessity in today's competitive work environment; it is also a vital component of effective time management. In your professional as well as your social life, the ability to remember names and faces; speak publicly without the need for written notes; and recall dates, appointments, and numbers can increase your productivity remarkably.

Much of your daily life revolves around memory. If you lost your memory, what would your life be like? If all you had was your autonomic responses, such as breathing, and your instinctual responses, such as eating and sex, what would your day be like?

You really wouldn't know what to wear or even what to have for breakfast, let alone how to prepare it. You would not remember what time to leave for work or even how a clock works. This, of course, wouldn't matter since you would also have forgotten what your job is as well as all the skills required to accomplish it.

If losing your memory would greatly diminish your effectiveness and have a negative impact on every aspect of your life, then the corollary is that improving your memory will greatly increase your effectiveness and have a positive impact on every aspect of your life, not just as a time manager but as a fully functioning, multifaceted human being.

According to John Orberg, author of the book *When the Game is Over It All Goes Back in the Box,* we spend (or more accurately, waste) roughly 16 minutes a day looking for our lost possessions. It's a sin of which we are all guilty—forgetting where we left the TV remote, or our glasses, or our car keys, and that document you know you filed last year.

Sometimes it's something more important than the TV remote. Yo-Yo Ma, the famed cellist, tells the story about getting into a cab in New York and putting his $2.5 million cello into the trunk. Arriving at his destination, he pays the cabbie, gets out of the cab, and walks off, leaving his cello in the trunk, not realizing until he gets into the hall what he has done.

Some people are plagued by misplaced treasures. My wife loves it when I tell the story of how she put a $20,000 ring in such a good hiding place that she never saw it again.

The term absentmindedness is an altogether appropriate term for this phenomenon because our minds' concentration is focused elsewhere, and not on the task at hand. If we can understand the causes of absentmindedness, then maybe we can eliminate it or, at least, greatly reduce its significance.

The first cause of absentmindedness is the lack of attention we're paying at the crucial moment, and the other involves how deeply we encode information.

There is a famous film clip that often shows up in Psychology 101 in which students are asked to watch a video of people passing a basketball between each other. They are then asked to count the number of passes. Then when it is finished, the participants are asked if they noticed anything unusual in the clip. Most of the students are rather puzzled by the question and say no. Then the experimenter replays the video clip, but this time, without them having to focus on counting the passes, everyone sees a person dressed like a gorilla walk right through the scene. It even smiles at the camera.

To a large extent, absentmindedness is a result of sensory overload. We live in a multitasking society in which too many things are happening at the same time and, not surprisingly, some of these things fall between the cracks. Also, the older we become and the busier we get with our careers and our families, the worse it becomes.

The second cause of absentmindedness relates to the depth at which we process information. If the encoding is too shallow, it will not take. Many people simply do not know how to increase the depth of their focus.

Many people confuse absentmindedness with a poor memory but they are really two different things.

Obviously, since the cause of much of our absentmindedness is the lack of original awareness, the solution is to increase and focus that awareness.

One way to do this is to tell yourself as you put the car keys on the coffee table, "I am putting my keys on the coffee table," or, as you leave your car in the car park, "I am parked by the exit door on the fourth floor." Better yet is to actually visualize the car keys on the coffee table, the same thing when you are placing a document in a file. When you place your glasses on the refrigerator, see a huge set of eye glasses on the refrigerator or when you place a document in a file folder say to yourself, "I am putting the Jones file back in its folder."

Also, if you have difficulty in this area, write it down or use a voice recorder. A young physicist once asked the great Albert Einstein for his telephone number. Einstein picked up the university telephone directory, located his number, scribbled it down on a piece of paper, and handed it to the young scientist. Bemused, the young man blurted out, "Mr. Einstein, don't you know your own phone number?" to which the great thinker replied, "Why should I clutter up my mind with something that I can so easily look up?"

Well, sometimes we cannot so easily look it up and, therefore, any improvement we can make will reap benefits.

The problem of absentmindedness is really one of inattention; your mind is literally absent when you perform a particular action.

One of the best ways to increase your ability to concentrate is to learn and practice mnemonic techniques. I have written a book called *Memory for Management* that presents practical systems for remembering names, faces, appointments, schedules, "to do" lists, and many other things.

As we advance in management, we are asked more and more often to speak publicly, which places increased demands on our time. Learning how to prepare a speech in a fraction of the time and how to deliver it confidently and without notes is an essential time management skill.

12. Procrastination

Lastly and appropriately, we come to procrastination.

Time management consultant R. Alec MacKenzie has suggested that of all management ills, procrastination looms as the most obvious and readily admitted. This time management problem affects us all to a greater or lesser degree. However, some people are more affected than others. Some joke about their procrastinating habit, kidding about having a lifetime membership in the "Procrastinator's Club," or quoting Mark Twain, "Never put off until tomorrow what you can do the day after tomorrow"; but it is really no joking matter. Relationships have failed because of procrastination, organizations have folded because of it, and people have died as a result of it.

To conquer procrastination, we must overcome our inertia, our tendency to resist taking action. From physics, we learn that a body remains at rest unless and until a force is exerted against it. Also, from physics we learn that it always takes less effort to sustain movement once inertia has been overcome.

What is Procrastination?

Simply put, procrastination is the avoidance of a task or project that needs to be accomplished. Procrastination is doing low-value tasks instead of critical ones. Procrastination is doing the urgent rather than the important. Procrastination is watching television when you should be exercising. Procrastination is enjoying a long lunch when things are stacked up back at the office. Procrastination is avoiding a person rather than facing him or her and resolving a problem. Procrastination is putting off that activity with your children because you have more important things to do.

According to noted psychologist Clarry Lay, procrastination occurs when there's "a temporal gap between intended behavior and enacted behavior." What he is saying is that procrastination occurs when there's a significant divide between when people intend to do a job, and when they actually do it.

Everyone procrastinates. Some do so occasionally, like the weekend warrior who works hard all week long just to spend his or her weekend in a cocaine high. They appear to function normally save perhaps an occasional lapse in judgment. This type of procrastinator rarely sees any reason to change. But like any addict, things always get worse and, in time, their procrastination becomes chronic.
The four most common tasks that cause us to procrastinate are:

1.   The unpleasant task
2.   The difficult or complex task
3.   The task that requires a decision
4.   The task that we see as inconsequential.

Everyone procrastinates with regard to their non-preferences. Each of the four behavioral styles is inclined to procrastinate when it comes to different things.

Dreamers, for example, have a bias for action and jump into a project with both feet. This penchant for quick action, however, only braces their tendency to procrastinate with regard to planning, goal setting, and other solitary activities. Also, as we have discussed earlier in this book, dreamers are unquestionably the most disorganized of the four behavioral styles. While they have the best intentions in the world, when it comes to actually attacking clutter and disorganization, it too often remains something that they plan to do one of these days. One of these days remains, too often, none of these days.

Supporters, on the other hand, tend to put off any type of confrontational situation. They know that other people tend to take advantage of them, and they hope to do something about it, but not right now. This struggle with conflict results in, and contributes to, their failure to say "no" to even the most selfish and unreasonable demands of others.

Thinkers procrastinate with regard to decision making. Thinkers, of course, don't view this as procrastination; to them, it is merely gathering enough information to make a well-informed and optimal decision.

Commanders procrastinate when it comes to delegation. While they often sense that someone else could perform many of the activities in which they are involved, they fear that it would take longer to explain how to perform the task to a subordinate than it would to complete the project themselves.

What are the Costs of Procrastination?

While the reasons for procrastination are numerous and varied, the costs of chronic procrastination are high and well defined. Procrastination can affect our relationships and our reputation. Others may view us as unreliable and undependable. It can affect our health, contributing to feelings of anxiety, frustration, and inadequacy, and significantly increase workplace stress, which is a major cause of poor time management.

In 2012, Americans overpaid their income taxes by almost $1 billion as a result of costly errors resulting from the rush to file before the deadline. Each year, we view television news reports of people queued up just before midnight, trying to get their tax return into the mailbox before the deadline. An increasing number of people file income tax extensions, not because they need additional information in order to complete their return, but because they leave it to the last minute. Some people put off filing taxes altogether and fall many years behind.

Many people put off retirement planning, waiting until their expenses are lower, their children are older, or the markets look better. They wait, but their retirement doesn't.

Procrastination can lead to a variety of physical and psychological problems, including depression, low self-esteem, and insomnia. Also, it can indirectly lead to illness and even premature death by discouraging visits to the doctor.

Procrastination can also threaten your happiness. The Procrastination Research Group at Carleton University in Canada surveyed 2,700 individuals asking the question, "To what extent is procrastination having a negative impact on youAlmost half (46%) said "quite a bit" or "very much," and almost one person in five

(18%) reported an "extreme negative effect."

But perhaps the greatest cost of procrastination is opportunity cost—books that go unwritten, graduations that never occur, careers that are never pursued, and loves that remain unrequited. "Procrastination is the grave in which opportunity is buried."

Why do People Procrastinate?

It is important to recognize that procrastination, like pain, is just a symptom. It is an effect rather than a cause and, like the symptom of pain, in order to deal with our procrastination habit, we first have to determine its cause.

There is no single answer to why people procrastinate; there are almost as many "whys" as there are "whats." However, the following are the most common:

- **Lack of self-discipline**
- **Lack of motivation**
- **The task is unpleasant**
- **The task appears too big**
- **Inability to make a decision**
- **Failure to set priorities**
- **A desire to do things perfectly**
- **Waiting for the perfect time**
- **Don't know where to start**
- **Fear of failure**
- **Fear of success**

Overcoming Procrastination

1. Identify your goals and objectives. The most fundamental reason we fail to start is that we don't know where we need to go. A major reason for procrastination is that we don't want to accomplish a goal enough to do everything that needs to be done to get started. Goals intensify our desire to achieve. Try to clarify what it is you hope to accomplish. Then once you have visualized what success looks like with regard to a particular project, like a good golfer, work back from the pin. Remember you can't "do" goals, you can only take actions. By identifying the steps or actions required to accomplish your goals, you have given substance to your desires. But identifying what you want to accomplish does not always suggest where you need to start. By working back for the successful completion it usually will become obvious If you cannot identify a clear entry point then just jump in. You will likely find a productive way forward.

2. Set a firm deadline. Deadlines create a sense of urgency. When we have a deadline for completion, it helps us to set priorities. In order to get things done, we need to set deadlines. Sometimes deadlines are set for us by others, sometimes they're not. If you are given an assignment without a deadline, set one. Remember what we learned from the activity matrix—human beings tend to respond to what is urgent, not necessarily what is important. If you want to write a novel, set a date for its publication.. If it's a new language that you are hoping to learn, plan a trip on a certain date in the future and set yourself the task of being fluent by that date. If you're planning for retirement, set a firm date for your retirement.

Deadlines are not frightening things. It's the way in which we deal with deadlines that sends us into a panic. Deadlines are really helpful tools that aid in our organization. Also, as with goals, we need to work backward from the final deadline. Break or divide your tasks and projects up into small steps, then decide how long you can spend of each of these steps and where you can fit them into your daily schedule.

3. Do the most unpleasant thing first. We all have a long list of unpleasantries that we would like to avoid: dental visits, pap smears, tax returns, an hour at the gym, closet reorganization, paying parking tickets, having dinner with the mother-in-law, just to mention a few.

Why not do these unpleasant things first and get them off your plates and off your mind? Often after you have completed an unpleasant task, you feel a sense of relief and satisfaction, and may even ask yourself, "Why didn't I take care of this thing long ago?" If you start your day this way, you will feel more relaxed, feel better about yourself, and the rest of your day will feel a lot lighter.

The great Mark Twain once quipped, "Eat a live frog first thing in the morning and nothing worse will happen to you the rest of the day."

I have an acquaintance by the name of Brian Tracy who is a prolific writer and speaker. We did our MBAs together in Canada. Brian has written a book entitled, *Eat That Frog*, which talks about the importance of this principle.

I would suggest the following for handling those chores and tasks that you hate:

- Try to find a way to make the chore or task more pleasant. Maybe you could play your favorite music while doing it or sip on a cappuccino if that's your thing. My housekeeper listens to talk radio while ironing.

- Break a big task down into smaller units. Don't clean out the entire garage; just do one cabinet or maybe just sweep it out today. Don't attack your office clutter all at once—maybe just one drawer today. I'll expand on this below.

- Set a time and stick to it. We can all do an unpleasant task for twenty minutes. Set a timer, work on it for twenty minutes, then leave it for the rest of that day.

- Give yourself a reward for the successful completion of the ugly task or activity. There's nothing wrong with bribing yourself to complete an unpleasant project. Promise yourself a reward for each part of the project that you complete. It might be something as simple as drinking a soda, going for a walk, or directing your attention to a project that you really enjoy. Psychologists call this operant conditioning. It's been shown that rewards reinforce behaviors and punishments discourage and extinguish behaviors. Celebrate that you've finally got it done!

Your mother was right after all when she insisted that you eat your
spinach first. If you attack the most unpleasant part of the task first,
the rest will be downhill.

4. Employ the Swiss cheese method. Break the object of your
procrastination down into smaller units. This is what Allan Lakein
calls the "Swiss cheese" method in his book, *How to Get Control of
Your Time and Your Life*. He says treat that large and overwhelming
task like a block of Swiss cheese. By gnawing a hole here and
gnawing a hole there, before you know it, you have reduced it to a
size that will enable you to gobble it all up. This is a good analogy
for the way in which we might deal effectively with those giant,
complex projects before us.

The accomplishment of great things always comes from the
accomplishment of many, many small things. Many times, we lose
track of that fact. We pull that enormous task out of our in-basket
and identify the scope and magnitude of the task, only to shove it
back in the pile, leaving it in abeyance while we do something that is
quicker, more fun, and easier. For this reason, I instruct people, as
they use their datebook organizers, not to write anything on their
prioritized daily "to do" list that will take them more than an hour.
If it will take more than an hour, it should be entered as two or
more individual tasks or actions. If, for example, it is going to take
you five hours to do a personnel planning report, it would be best to
enter this on your list as a number of individual tasks to probably be
completed over a number of days, such as:

- Gather required documentation
- Prepare the outline
- Write the objectives, etc.

Tasks are overwhelming because of their size, complexity, or the amount of time involved in their completion. By breaking down a task into sub-units, we provide structure for ourselves and we reduce complexity.

5. Strive for excellence, not perfection. Perfectionism is the handmaiden of procrastination. The desire to do things perfectly every time is a major cause of procrastination. It is important then for you not to become obsessed with doing every job perfectly.

Thinkers and commanders both have difficulty here; they would rather put things off than do them in an imperfect manner. Sometimes this is laudable and altogether appropriate but, more often, this high standard is applied to tasks and undertakings for which perfection is unnecessary and our desire to achieve it too often means that we do nothing.

Just begin and work steadily; the aim is progress not perfection. If necessary or appropriate, you can always go back later and revise, edit, amend, and expand, but at least you have something that you can go back and polish.

6. Shout it from the rooftops. Let others know about your deadline and commitment. We may frequently break commitments we make to ourselves, but we are far less likely to break commitments that we make or share with other people. It can be painful and embarrassing to have to admit to others that we have failed. Get someone to hold you accountable. It's easy to feel alone with your problems. Have someone check up on you during certain intervals.

Organizations such as Alcoholics Anonymous, Narcotics Anonymous, and Weight Watchers, as well as a myriad of other

---

highly successful twelve-step and self-help groups have recognized this principle. They all require you to make a group commitment to change. By making a public commitment, you are less likely to procrastinate; so make a pledge to your boss, spouse, or friend.

Make a commitment to strengthen your resolve. Take some time to analyze your procrastinating habit. Ask yourself the following six questions:

1. What things do I tend to put off most often?

2. What am I putting off right now?

3. How do I feel about my procrastination habit?

4. What has my procrastination cost me?

5. What do I feel is the cause of most of my procrastination?

6. What can I do to overcome my procrastination?

If you can master your procrastination, you have gone a long way toward the management of your time, for, contrary to conventional wisdom, it is the internal time wasters—our inability to say no, our own personal lack of organization, and our habit of procrastinating—that are our greatest time thieves. The steps I have outlined above will help you to overcome your inertia and gain greater control of yourself, your time, and your life.

> "The best time to plant a tree was twenty years ago. The second best time is now."
>
> Chinese Proverb

Chapter 9

Interacting with the Four Styles

The Dreamer

In your interactions with dreamers, it is important to try to match their fast pace. Speak quickly, respond to their questions quickly, and try as best you can to be lively and entertaining, even charming.

It is well worth your time to build personal rapport.

It is important to recognize that with regard to dreamers, and indeed all styles, their core behaviors are well established and largely unchangeable. It falls on you then to accept, with as much patience as you can muster, their spontaneity and impulsive nature. Try to consider various options and approaches that can accommodate the dreamer's modus while still serving your needs and those of the organization.

It is wise, for example, to actually budget time for personal stories, jokes, anecdotes, and social interaction.

Remember, too, that dreamers procrastinate more than the other styles. This can certainly be problematic when your work depends on their input. Their tendency to put things off is partly a result of their tendency to take on so much, not incidentally because they cannot say "no," but because they want to be aware of and involved in everything. It also results from their lack of planning. As we said earlier, dreamers have a bias for action; they jump in with both feet absent adequate planning. They also accept too many interruptions.

Any action, then, that you can take that engages dreamers in planning is beneficial and will, over time, reduce the impact of their innate behaviors.

A general rule is that we should seek to move inflexible and controlling individuals toward greater flexibility and help to find ways for flexible individuals to gain greater control and structure in terms of the use of their time.

If you can help them to overcome their natural inertia with perhaps team or "group start" activities, you may find that not only will they accomplish a great deal in a relatively short period
of time, but they will also inspire and motivate others to do likewise.

Recognize, too, that the dreamer also tends to become easily bored, particularly when a project tends to bog him or her down, resulting in a tendency to jump from one task or project to another. Your awareness of this reality and your personal involvement in seeking to motivate and re-energize the dreamer is vital.

Speak to dreamers' future-oriented approach rather than focusing too much on plans and schedules or involving them in what they see as minutiae.

The Supporter

Take the time to show a personal interest in supporters and when you disagree with them, discuss feelings as well as facts.

Supporters tend to procrastinate with respect to confrontational situations. Their fear of offending others often limits their effectiveness, and their inability to say "no" results in them being overwhelmed.

It is vital that you set specific goals in consultation with them because of their tendency to be cooped by others or pressured to accept other persons' goals as their own. Supporters' concern with relationships, coupled with their inability to say "no," often results in misdirected effort. While their organizational skills are good, they tend to facilitate other people's goals to the detriment of their own. Indicate to them the importance and priority of the assignment given and ask them to run the requests of others, or any demand on their time by others, past you first.

Seek to get "buy in" as best you can, but recognize, too, that supporters do not always communicate directly. They need to be encouraged to be honest in terms of their commitment to any assignment that you give to them. They will often indicate agreement or display tacit support, not wanting to upset you or create conflict.

When delegating to supporters, appeal to their sense of group commitment. Remember that relationships matter the most to supporters. If you seek commitment from them in a group context, you will more likely see more positive results than if you make a personal or private request of them.

Also listen to supporters. Their communication is again indirect and you often need to read between the lines. Clarify and paraphrase. Try to extract the true feelings, mindset, and meaning behind the words.

To motivate supporters, show them how their actions, the actions you are proposing, will benefit their relationships, not how they will have more power or money of greater visibility.

Try to match their relaxed pace and stick with familiar ways of doing things. Show a personal interest in them.

You will create friction with supporters by getting right down to business without the social niceties, making unilateral decisions without allowing everyone to be heard, or forcing them to participate in a group situation in a manner in which they find threatening.

The Thinker

Because of the high standards that thinkers set for themselves and their tendency toward perfectionism, they may spend an inordinate amount of time on relatively unimportant matters or doing everything in which they are involved at an unnecessary level of precision. For this reason, it is critical that you place time limits on assignments given and set clear priorities on projects and assignments.

It can help to pair the perfectionistic thinker up with someone who has a more realistic view of the relative value of each project.

The way in which you react or respond to any mistake that a thinker makes can either contribute to or diminish his or her perfectionistic tendencies. Forgive and forget flaws or the occasional mistake.

Thinkers do not see meetings as the best use of their time and, in fact, they probably are not. The strength of thinkers' approach comes from their ability to solve problems in a thorough and comprehensive manner. Meetings, therefore, particularly meetings that have devolved into information-sharing sessions, often create stress and impatience in the thinker.

In addition to trying to improve your meetings, one technique that often helps is to engage thinkers in the process by having them present progress reports on the assignments that they have been given or the project with which they are currently involved. Be careful not to put them on the spot, however, as they often feel less comfortable in group situations.

Also provide time in the meeting for proper analysis and questions because thinkers will always have some. Try to answer their questions even though you may think that they are unnecessary or irrelevant. Focus on facts rather than opinions and set and move the agenda forward in a linear or sequential manner. Try to minimize personal stories and anecdotes in the meeting and stay on topic. Remember, too, that making decisions too quickly or based on emotion leaves the thinker cold.

Thinkers also tend to procrastinate with regard to decision making. This stems, in part, from their mistaken belief that more information and data will ensure a better decision and subsequent outcome. While it is true that good information is vital to good decisions, there is also a point of diminishing returns where additional information does not justify the cost of its acquisition.

This constant quest for more and better information is another manifestation of their perfectionistic tendencies.

Remember that decision making involves making a choice and selecting from amongst alternatives. Therefore, if you can find ways to reduce the number of alternatives, you can at least improve the speed with which thinkers can make a decision. This may mean stepping in at an appropriate time and, in consultation with them, eliminating certain alternatives or lines of enquiry. Be sure to also praise the speed with which they are able to produce excellent results.

The Commander

In interacting with the commander try not to focus too much on process. Discuss and debate outcomes, not procedures, and argue the facts, not your personal opinions. Lengthy discussion of alternatives and detailed data analysis leaves the commander cold. Rather, try to focus on the big picture and the bottom line.

Commanders are more concerned with where we are going than how we are going to get there. Provide actions and alternatives for decision making and give recognition to their goals and objectives.

When delegating to them, give them the bottom line and get out of their way.

Once you have delegated a project to them, don't hang over them observing their progress. Commanders are typically intelligent, motivated individuals and, given a clear set of goals and the tools necessary to accomplish the job, they will usually come through for you.

Try to be precise and, above all, be on time. For commanders, every minute counts and they do not like them to be wasted. Cut to the chase and try as best as possible to match their fast pace.

Commanders don't see meetings as the best use of their time and when they chair them, they often do so with military precision, which tends to limit valuable input and discussion. Recognize this tendency and always add a discussion section to the written agenda when a commander is chairing.

Try to keep the meeting on course and avoid storytelling, brainstorming, or the use of emotional appeals.

Unlike the thinker, who labors over every decision, the commander makes rapid, almost snap decisions, which are often good but could, in some cases, be improved if other ideas and opinions were to be tabled.

Commanders have trouble delegating. This comes from their fear of other people's incompetence. They feel that no one else can do the job as well as they can. They say to themselves, "It would take me as long to explain this project and the issues associated with it as it would for me to do it myself. Besides, they wouldn't do it as well as I could." This is probably altogether true—it will take as long and it is likely that the delegate will not do the job as well as the commander could *this time*; but if they don't take the time to delegate, they will never truly have a team.

The commander is allergic to detail and, for that reason, tends to procrastinate when it comes to routine and inconsequential activities. Commanders also tend to spend too much of their valuable time on less critical aspects of important tasks because of their failure to delegate.

Concluding Comments

*What a piece of work is a man, how noble in reason, how infinite in faculties, in
form and moving how express and admirable, in action how like an angel, in
apprehension how like a god! the beauty of the world, the paragon of animals...*

Hamlet Act 2, scene 2

You are a remarkable individual. You have tremendous skills and
unlimited potential. But you are and will always be an individual –
not a team, not a group, not a company, not a church - an
individual. You are unique, a separate thing.

Your uniqueness is a blessing, but in modern organizational life it
can also be a curse. There are many features of your personality and
behavioral style that fit well and contribute to the needs of your
organization; but there are also things about you that do not fit well
or enhance the collective.

Your success and ultimately your happiness in today's workplace
very much depends on your ability to adapt. To modify your
instinctive behaviors so as to better sync with those of your
colleagues and better suit the requirements of your organization.

There is no area where this is truer than that of time-management.
Good time-management is a learned behavior. There are many time-
tested skills and techniques that can help you accomplish more and
actually feel less stressed while doing so. Some of these skills and
techniques might come naturally to you, others, seem extremely
foreign. The important thing is that you find a way to integrate the

most important of these techniques with your natural and unique behavioral style.

This has been the goal of this book. To firstly make you aware of your distinctive time-style and secondly to provide you with practical advice for drawing on as well as modifying your natural behavioral tendencies so as to accomplish more while reducing stress.

I hope that this book will contribute to even greater success in your life and career.

Appendices

Appendix A

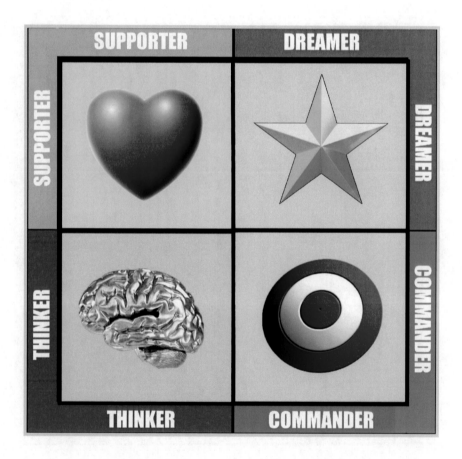

Appendix B

Behavioral Styles Matrix

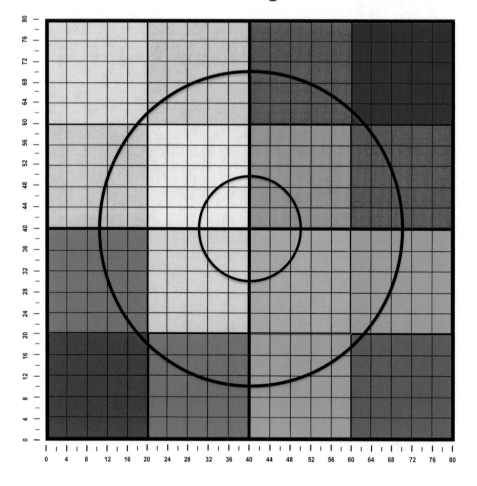

Appendix C

Time-Style Problem Identification Chart

	Dreamer	Supporter	Thinker	Commander
Planning & Prioritization	Often	Often	Occasionally	Often
Organizing	Often	Occasionally	Occasionally	Occasionally
Socializing Interruptions	Often	Often	Occasionally	Often
The Telephone	Often	Often	Often	Often
Email & Internet	Often	Often	Often	Occasionally
Handling Paperwork	Often	Occasionally	Often	Occasionally
Meetings	Occasionally	Often	Often	Often
Delegation	Occasionally	Often	Often	Often
Perfectionism	Often	Often	Often	Often
Unable to Say "No"	Often	Often	Occasionally	Often
Focus & Forgetfulness	Often	Often	Often	Often
Procrastination	Often	Often	Often	Often

- Seldom a Problem Area for You
- Occasionally a Problem Area for You
- Often a Problem Area for You

Index